A SAHAJ MARG COMPANION

THE NATURAL PATH

Shri Parthasarathi Rajagopalachari with the author.
Coimbatore, India
March 1993

A Sahaj Marg Companion

The Natural Path

Clark Powell

Shri Ram Chandra Mission

USA

Shri Ram Chandra Mission
Post Office Box 269
Molena, GA 30258
U.S.A.
http://www.srcm.org

First edition: August 1996
First paperback edition: October 2000

ISBN 0-945242-54-9 (paperback)

ISBN 0-945242-31-X

Hear now the wisdom of Yoga, the path
of the Eternal and freedom from bondage.

No step is lost on this path, and no dangers are found.
And even a little progress is freedom from fear.

Bhagavad Gita

CONTENTS

PREFACE

This book, I pray, will be useful not only to those already practicing the Raja Yoga method known as Sahaj Marg (pronounced *Sa-hazh Marg*, with a hard "g" as in God), but also to anyone interested in spiritual adventure. For readers who have never heard of Sahaj Marg, which means Natural Path or Simple Way, this book may serve as an introduction; however, three points need to be clarified for anyone encountering Sahaj Marg for the first time through these pages.

First, this book is simply an introduction. To appreciate the breadth and depth of Sahaj Marg philosophy and psychology, the reader is referred to the books of the Masters. A listing of the growing body of Sahaj Marg literature in various languages is available from the training centers listed at the end of the book.

Second, just as reading a menu can indicate what is available yet can never substitute for actually tasting the meal, neither can reading this nor any other book convey what may only be revealed through the actual practice of Sahaj Marg. As Babuji used to say, "Read and enjoy; do and become." Sahaj Marg is a very practical and pragmatic approach to spiritual realization. We are asked not to believe in doctrines, but to observe our own experience; not to trust secondhand information, but to test for ourselves by direct experiment. Those who wish to move beyond reading about Sahaj Marg and would like to experience the method for themselves are welcome to do so. If after reading something about the practice you are willing to give it your best effort for at least three to six months, you may then judge the practical results for yourself, and decide if you wish to continue. To begin, simply contact one of the centers for the addresses of the preceptors living nearest to you.

Third, the life of the practice, as you will see, flows from heart to heart through direct yogic transmission. Thus, to truly practice Sahaj Marg, it is essential to contact a preceptor so that this connection can be established. Those who attempt to practice the techniques described in this book on their own are likely to be disappointed. The reasons for this are discussed in the section titled "Beginning Sahaj Marg," and other hints about starting Sahaj Marg (or any spiritual practice, for that matter) are scattered throughout the book.

For *abhyasis* — that is, for those who are already doing the *abhyas* or practice of Sahaj Marg — this book will have another use. Hopefully, it may serve as a companion to their practice, as a reminder and reference for experienced abhyasis, and as a clarification for many of the concerns frequently raised by new abhyasis.

The format of this book was modeled after A.P. Durai's concise and practical *Basics of Sahaj Marg Sadhana: Questions and Answers*, which was originally published in India in 1991. I felt that an expanded version would be helpful, one written especially to reflect the kinds of questions often raised by Europeans and Americans. When I discovered that S. Krishna Sai and Victor Kannan, two Indian preceptors of Sahaj Marg living in the United States, had made a list of FAQ's ("frequently asked questions") I called them and we began to collaborate on what was originally to be simply a photocopied pamphlet.

The first questions we collected were the ones we kept hearing again and again from those who showed up at the informal "Open Houses" held to introduce Sahaj Marg in the West, and also from new abhyasis. These questions were primarily about the practice. We did not want to repeat the able work of A.P. Durai, and if a question touched on grounds he had already covered, we tried to approach it from the different angle of the Western mind.

Yet as I began writing and then re-writing, our "pamphlet" kept growing because more questions kept arising from the responses given. In each succeeding draft, the scope of the questions widened from those about the practice to those of a more psychological or philosophical nature, the only requirement being that the question was at some level, or for some people, vital to the spiritual endeavor. Eventually they became the questions I was wondering about myself, and the answers that surfaced often surprised me. They seemed to come from somewhere beyond my current understanding.

Receiving answers in this manner is not unusual in Sahaj Marg, nor is having those answers turned back into questions, as I have learned. For instance, once in a garden near Calcutta, Chariji called me over to him. "Okay, Mr. Journalist," he said, "do you have any questions?"

I looked within. At that particular moment, I found I had no thoughts, and no questions. I had nothing in my mind and nothing in my heart but happiness at sitting in a garden at the feet of the Master. "No Sir," I said. "No questions."

Chariji gave one of his little Yoda-like snorts. Silence. Then all of a sudden, a series of questions began to stream into my mind. I felt that maybe they were the questions in the minds of the hundred or so abhyasis sitting around us. This wasn't the first time I had this uncanny sense, and I wanted to ask Master about it.

"Sir," I said, "sometimes I have the feeling that the questions I'm always asking you don't come from me. I mean, they don't seem to belong to me at all."

Chari nodded. "That is a correct feeling," he said. "You see, sometimes when the Source wishes to give an answer, but hesitates because no question has yet been asked, then It will generate questions too."

The latest example happened just the other day. I had gone up to the Shri Ram Chandra Mission Ashram near Atlanta for the weekend, taking along a draft of this manuscript for my friends to proof and correct. Since my wife and I arrived late and since a draft needed to be ready in five days to be taken to Madras by an abhyasi who was leaving for India, about eight of us stayed up all night to get the work done. Assisted by two batches of *chai*, the first editing job was completed just before dawn. As we left, I was saying that it would be nice if Chariji would provide some kind of Introduction.

A few hours later, all of us came to the morning *satsangh*, or morning meditation, looking a little bedraggled to say the least. A preceptor from Dallas led the meditation, which was quite light and restful. Afterwards this preceptor was asked to read something, and so he walked over to a table, picked up the first book he saw and opened it. Our friend, who knew nothing of the book we'd been working on, had chosen at random a talk given by Chariji a few years ago and collected in *Heart to Heart: Volume II.* As he began to read, I glanced at those who had heard me wish aloud a few hours earlier that Master would provide an Introduction. They were smiling. The talk read that morning appears in this book as "The Right Question."

◆ ◆ ◆

Among Babuji's now-famous sayings was his description of the ideal *abhyasi* (as anyone who follows the *abhyas* or practice of Sahaj Marg is called). He said that such a person would have "an Eastern heart and a Western mind." Indians generally have a sweetness of spirit and a natural devotion that amazes most Westerners, who are comparatively analytical and pragmatic, and tend to approach spiritual matters with a lively skepticism or even wary suspicion. Westerners often like to ask blunt and direct questions. I have tried to include in this book every question of current or vital interest to Westerners I could think of, and not to avoid subjects that may be difficult or challenging.

Spiritual seekers deserve to have their concerns met clearly and openly, and should know right from the start what is expected of them. A few years ago, Chariji said: "I believe that we do those who come to us a disservice if we water down the system of Sahaj Marg, thinking that if we make it sound easy, they will become abhyasis, and that once they have become abhyasis, they will remain. It is the wrong way of tackling the situation. We should tell the most difficult thing first. Then a person understands that if he wants a destiny which is different from the run-of-the-mill destiny, he has to do something different for it. There is no objection to your remaining human, if that is the destiny you wish. There is no enforcement of any ritual or practice or discipline in Sahaj Marg. Sahaj Marg only says that if you want to be this, and this, and this, then this you must do."

Doubtless there will be more questions that could have been included, just as I am certain that often the responses fail to reflect the deep wisdom and humor that Chariji would display if you were lucky enough to be sitting at his feet and could fling the question directly at him. His answers are often quite funny, and come with surprising brevity, and the typical experience on hearing them is to think, "Well, of course. I knew that!"

And you do know it. One thing we learn quickly when we come to Master is that the only answers that matter are the answers that come from our own heart. You will find nothing in this book, if it is deep and true enough, that you do not already know, for at the level of the original Spirit, we do not need to be informed, but reminded.

As the Masters tell us, truth can never be absorbed merely from question-and-answer sessions. Only our own direct perception of the Real can supply this. If this book can only help satisfy a few itches of the mind, and put one or two concerns to rest so that we can stop relentlessly asking and answering someone "out there" and get on with the Real Work, then it will have served its purpose. Many of us, myself included, have had the experience of approaching the Master bristling with all sorts of questions, only to find that in His presence we forget everything we wanted to ask, or that the questions now seem irrelevant and needless.

When the bee is flying about, it buzzes, but when it finds the nectar in the flower, it becomes silent. Just so, Babuji described the Master as a "silencer." So this book is aimed at the Silence-within-Silence, a state far beyond any possibility of a question or an answer, and one that a capable Master may introduce with a mere smile, if our hearts are ready for it.

May the questions and the quest continue. If there are future editions of *A Sahaj Marg Companion: The Natural Path*, perhaps these might reflect an ongoing journey in which questions change, and answers, too.

I would like to thank all the friends who helped bring this book to you. First, heartfelt thanks to Sai and Kannan, whose initial encouragement and considerable contributions gave the project its birth. To Stone, Wren, Murali, Balaji, Christine, Diana, Bill, Don, and to my wife Sondra for their critiques. To Alexey, Christopher, Sanjay, Santosh, Bhoopathi, and Charlie for their technical assistance, and to Barbara Jean, Teresa, and Kirstin for their insights regarding women and spirituality.

And of course, to my Master, whose light hand guided the entire development of this book. Without Chariji's review and approval of every sentence, I would never dare to write a book about Sahaj Marg, which to me is now more a mystery than ever.

Sahaj Marg is a path that has no surface, a practice whose habitat is Infinity. Like a diamond cut by a master jeweler, which reveals unanticipated depths of intricate splendor as one turns it in the light and gazes into its facets, so Sahaj Marg is a continuous surprise and an endless adventure. I do not presume to understand much about it. These days, the word that best conveys my grasp of Sahaj Marg is *wonder*.

For all its inadequacies, I humbly offer this little book to the only real Companion I have ever found, my Master, Pujya Shri Parthasarathi Rajagopalachariji Maharaj, with the prayer that His blessing may overcome its limits and touch all who read these pages.

— Clark Powell

January 25, 1996
Basant Panchami

A SAHAJ MARG COMPANION

THE NATURAL PATH

Introduction: The Right Question

Parthasarathi Rajagopalachari

Informal talk given 5 September 1987 at Bonascre, France

For the past three days we have been having interviews with abhyasis. François will confirm that wherever the interviews were delayed, the people came back and said they had already found the answer in meditation, or from inside. I mean, there were so many cases yesterday, today, day before yesterday. So the real source of the answer is here inside us. What makes us ask questions and suffer until we get an answer is our impatience. So the basic problem about these questions is our urgency as we conceive it, you see. I have a question now, I must have an answer now, and I refuse to wait. So this is the problem, and if we are wise you know the old English saying, Sleep over it! The answer comes. So, don't unnecessarily be worried about these questions; most of them have no relevance to our existence. We must remember that human beings have lived for hundreds of thousands of years, and for most of that time nobody asked any questions. They just existed.

This business of questions and answers is a phenomenon of the intellect. A typical modern disease, because we don't know even what questions to ask sometimes. Because there are vital questions and there are irrelevant questions. What is a vital question? Well, if you take a primitive society when a man had to kill something to eat, the vital question was where to find the animal and how to shoot it or kill it, not about how the animals came and, you know, Genesis. I think that old saying that "Satan finds mischief for idle hands to do," can be rephrased for modern times, "Satan finds questions for idle minds to ask"! Because when we are fully occupied we have no questions. It's a fact. We all know it. Very often I have found, in the time of my Master and now, it is the people who don't meditate who want to know how to meditate. It is the people who don't clean themselves who are worried about blockages and grossness.

So the true answer to our questions is not answers, but doing. How to cook: suppose your daughter asks how to cook. You don't give a lecture on how to light the fire and put the vessel on the fire and put water into it and pour barley into it; you do it and show her how to do it. So practical questions can be answered by doing things for you and showing how it is to be done.

That is what the Master does. He delays the answer, gives you the time to meditate, does a little cleaning and removes the question from your mind. It is not that you find an answer — that is not quite correct. The question ceases to interest us. Very often people come and say, "Oh, I found the answer this morning in meditation." It is my experience that the answer was a change in the abhyasi's condition. This is what you have all found when you were with Babuji Maharaj; that we went with volumes and volumes of questions to ask, and when we went into his presence we forgot all the questions. Most of us didn't remember to ask any questions until we came back, then we said, Oh, I had so many questions to ask, but I didn't ask any of them!

Now, why didn't we ask those questions? Because when we were there, in the presence of the Master, it was like wet cloth drying before the sun — the questions evaporated. Our condition was changed, and it is like the cloth which says, "Oh, how did I become dry? I just came to become dry, and I became dry." This is the problem with questions, you see, that they come from the intellect and trouble us because we seek understanding rather than results. What is the use of a sick person understanding his disease? What he wants is a cure. You know, often you find troublesome patients in doctors' clinics. They not only want to be cured, but they want to know all the answers. They waste the doctor's time.

So we must make sure that we get what we need, not what we ask for. Not because we have no right to ask for, but because we don't know what to ask for. So Babuji always used to say, "Please ask only practical questions."

He was always amused when people came to him and asked, "Does God exist?" He said, "What a funny question these people ask." Because philosophy also says, if it was not existing, you couldn't ask of a thing whether it exists or not. The fact that you can ask the question, "Does God exist?" proves that God exists.

So Master used to advise: "Don't waste your time asking foolish questions, try to realize His presence." That is why he was against the phrase "searching for God." Because you can only search for something you have lost. God cannot ever be lost. God is not something like that. We may have lost Him, you see, in the sense that we have become isolated in our consciousness, and are suffering because of that isolation. It is like a man shutting himself up in a room and saying, "There is no air, there is no air!" Open the windows!

So all that we need to get answers to our questions is to open the windows of our soul, you see, and receive, not answers, but grace. So please remember this for the future regarding questions.

The second thing is, in the last two days I have had a host of people coming to me with the complaint that there is a blockage in their heart. Now there is one thing we must understand. There cannot possibly be anything inside me which some outer or external agency has put inside. We must have done it ourselves. Now, if it is not a physical thing, like bad food or bad water, it must be mental. So most of these blocks that we feel are mental blocks. So we have to clean and remove it. Then they say, "Oh, it is so bad, I am not able to even meditate." It is as if ... what shall I say ... as tragic, as comic, as a sick man saying, "I am too sick to take medicine." It has got to be done. And very often people come and say, "Oh, you know, I haven't been able to meditate for one year, and I have no results." This is an even bigger contradiction, that we expect results without doing anything. I mean, these are all the experiences of the last two, three days, and it is causing me much, what should I say, sorrow. That abhyasis don't meditate for two years, and then complain that they have no results!

When you ask them why they don't meditate, they say they feel blocked. How did this block come? "Maybe I did something wrong." Are you continuing to do it wrong now?

"Yes, unfortunately." (laughter) Why do you continue to do it? "Because I am not meditating." (laughter)

You see it goes round and round in circles. So what should we do about these things? After all, we are asked to meditate a maximum of one hour in the morning; thirty minutes cleaning in the evening and ten minutes prayer at night. We don't have the time for this. Or we don't have the inclination for it. One abhyasi came and told me that every time he wanted to meditate he found something else to do! Now, how is it possible to find something else to do, when you have something to do already? It only means the mind is not on meditation. So the only remedy was to advise him, "Please do it."

So you see how ridiculous this situation is, that we create all these problems by misunderstanding, by misapplication of the will. Because there is one thing which Babuji always used to emphasize: that if you have the will power to apply at all, to anything, it must be applicable to anything that you want to do. So if you cannot do one thing and can do another thing with the same will power, it only means that you want to do one thing while you don't want to do the other. The will power is not lacking and is not to be blamed.

So you see, essentially the inability to meditate is not really an inability to meditate, but an unwillingness to meditate. Babuji has told so many abhyasis in my presence, "If my meditating for you could benefit, I would do the meditation also for you gladly." But it is as silly as saying, "If I could eat for you, I would eat for you." You must eat. So please try to understand this: that whenever we say we can't meditate, we don't want to meditate. Because there is nothing in nature which can oppose a determined will. And what is necessary is to reassign our priorities, and do the meditation.

If you do this, you will find there are no more questions, the path to the goal becomes smooth and progress is assured.

The second thing about questions I have also referred to in the past is that they are generally desire-based. So whichever way you look at it, a question has no meaning. That is why we try to avoid answering questions immediately. And intellectual answers have no relevance to our life. I remember Babuji once answered a young man who asked him the question "Does God exist?" Babuji asked him, "Suppose I say, Yes. Will you accept it?" Then I said, "Why do you ask him this question?" He told me, "This boy must have asked this question of a hundred people already. And whether I say, 'Yes, God exists,' or 'No, God does not exist,' it conveys nothing to him." So you see the fact that a question is answered need not convey anything to us automatically.

One man came to me, who was a troublesome prospective abhyasi, very argumentative. He asked me a question. He said, "Are you a fool?"

I said, "Yes, of course I am." (laughter)

Then he said, "How can you answer like this?"

I said, "When you ask me a question, I answer the truth."

He said, "No, no, but you are in this position in which your Master has placed you, how can you give such an answer?"

I then asked him, "What answer did you expect?"

He said, "I thought you would say, 'No, I am wise' and I would have said, 'You are a damn fool.'"

So I told him, "I have saved you that trouble." You know, the surprising thing was that he was so impressed he became an abhyasi. So what was it that impressed him? What was it that impressed him with the answer? A twist of the intellect, that's all.

Why I am giving this example is to show you another facet of human behavior. The questioner is not necessarily impressed with the answer. They are generally impressed with the way in which it is answered. That is why if somebody asks, "Does God exist?" and you say, "Yes," he gets up and goes away. But if you sit for three hours and talk of Kant and Schopenhauer and Nietzsche and all this nonsense, without answering his question, he is very impressed. So they don't want answers, they are really testing your knowledge.

A Master has a right to refuse to have his knowledge tested. Or at least you should be capable of testing it in the right way. So I think generally these Masters like my Master, Babuji, or Lalaji — it is not that they don't want to answer our questions. They are waiting for the right question to come, which will really prove to them that here is a man who can test my knowledge, test my capacity, test my spiritual approach. And then they will probably hug us and accept us.

It is said, "Know a man by the questions he asks." That is why Babuji used to be disgusted with people who asked very lewd questions, low questions, you know, at the lowest level of existence — questions about sex and this and that. He was disgusted not because he was a prude, or because the subject is dirty. He was sad that a human being who should think of something high is thinking of something so low. That you should go to a Master and ask such questions this was his sadness. I know many people misunderstood it and said, "Aha, these Hindus, you know, they have a closed mind about sex." It is stupid. I have said, I think in another context in another place, that if you want to really know about sex, go to a Hindu. The Europeans don't know even the first thing about it yet. I mean, the Hindus have written books thousands of years ago about sex which haven't been discovered here yet. So it was not prudery. It was not any sort of unwillingness to talk about this subject. It was sorrow. It would have been like going to Einstein, for instance, and saying, What is two plus three equal to? Or going to God and asking for a packet of peanuts.

So that was my Master's sorrow; not unwillingness to answer questions or to be asked questions, but the tragedy of his own existence in that here is a storehouse of divinity, and people come with nothing more than the interest like rats have to nibble at a piece of cheese. Of course, I don't suppose that tragedy can be easily removed. Because they (people like the Masters) are from such a high descent it would not be, perhaps, possible to find any single questioner who could ask them the question that they are waiting for. So that is why I have referred to a Master's life as a tragic life in this sense. Those of you who are parents know how delighted you are when your child asks an intelligent question. Why are you delighted? And why are you annoyed when the child asks a stupid question? It is the same thing that happens to the Master. We are all his children and he expects at least once in a way an intelligent question from us. But, unfortunately, such masters are doomed to disappointment, I think most of the time. Even Einstein has said that it's not necessary to know the right answers, but it is necessary to know the right questions.

So if you want something from the Master, know what to ask for. And I will assure you it is one of the most difficult things on earth, because it is not a matter of knowledge, it is not a matter of search, of the intellect, of race or consciousness or anything like that. It is a question of the yearning of the heart. When that yearning is there, you know what to ask the Master. Not what I want, what I want to change, how to get rid of my headache, how to get this done, whether I should move my house or not.

But such a person would go straight to the Master and say, "Master, I have one thing to ask of you."

And the Master may say, "Yes, what is it?"

And this man should be able to say, "I want you."

That is the only thing.

PART ONE

QUESTIONS

THE GOAL

What does "Sahaj Marg" mean? What is Sahaj Marg?

The Sanskrit *sahaj* may be translated as natural, simple, or spontaneous and *marg* or *marga* means way or path. Sahaj Marg means the Natural Path, or Simple Way.

Sahaj Marg is a way of life designed to give the direct experience of Realization in the midst of daily life. Sahaj Marg emphasizes that Realization is for everyone, not just for monks or nuns. Indeed, family life in one's own home is an excellent means of learning real lessons about sacrifice and love. Sahaj Marg suggests that the highest spiritual attainments can be realized by anyone at any time in any place and does not accept the romantic notion that to realize God or Self we must renounce society or adopt arduous practices. Divinity dwells not in the Himalayas, but in the human heart. Sahaj Marg says that God is simple, and may be approached by simple means.

What is the goal of Sahaj Marg practice?

We respectfully submit that the goal of Sahaj Marg is the goal of human life.

This Goal has been given many different names by the great spiritual traditions, yet it does not matter what words we use to refer to the one Goal they all share. Whether we choose to call it enlightenment, or *moksha*, or becoming one with God, we are finally attempting to describe the indescribable, a stage far beyond the limits of any language.

The actual possibility of becoming one with God or Self is thought to be the highest imaginable attainment for any human being, and with God's grace, it is actually attainable by all His children. Whether we realize it consciously or not, all of us have taken human birth so that we might realize and express our Original Nature, which is Divine. There is no purpose for human life beyond this. In Sahaj Marg the means toward this end is meditation, which regulates the mind, and cleaning, which removes the past impressions and clears the hurdles in the path, made possible by the indispensable divine grace which the spiritual guide or Master pours into the heart of the practitioner through *pranahuti* or transmission.

Why must there be a "goal" for a spiritual practice? The Buddhists say that the yearning for enlightenment is itself a bar to enlightenment, and didn't even Lord Krishna say in the Gita that we should act, but take no thought for the fruit or reward of that action?

This is correct. In Sahaj Marg, we do not think of the Goal as some kind of external reward to be achieved, or faraway destination to be attained, or boon to be awarded by some Guru to those who have met a set of conditions or passed a test. Desiring a "goal" or some "other" state of being in this way is indeed a mistaken idea for any spiritual aspirant, and as the second line of the Mission Prayer indicates, ironically misses the whole point of the practice of Sahaj Marg.

Nonetheless, we do practice, just as Buddhists and Karma Yogis do. The State or Goal we approach is within, and has always been with us — it is none other than our own Original Nature. It might be said that practice is not for attaining something we do not already possess, but for removing that which blocks our realization of the Original Condition which we have forgotten, but which has always been ours. But mere intellectual appreciation of this goal-less Goal is nothing like the full realization of it to the depths of our being; it is the difference between, say, holding a blueprint of an ancient and vanished palace and living as a king in that palace. Thus, we practice.

And our practice simply makes us more adept at journeying. The difference between one who practices and one who does not is like the difference between a traveler and a lost person. The first has an idea of where he or she is going, and the best way to go; the latter is aimlessly wandering and, beyond a vague misgiving, may not even realize he or she is lost.

Finally, Sahaj Marg understands that this ultimate Goal has the nature of Infinity, and really speaking there is never any reaching of such a Goal. Even Lalaji, the Samarth Guru Mahatma Ram Chandraji of Fatehgarh, is said to be still "swimming toward the Center." As Lalaji expressed the view from the pinnacle of superconsciousness: "The search for

God and Soul...is imbecility. This fantasy is cured by another fantasy who is Guru."

But isn't going to Heaven or liberation from rebirth the goal of human life?

As for going to Heaven when we die, this is a matter for religion to debate. Sahaj Marg takes the view of Christ, that the kingdom of God is within. Union with God is far beyond popular notions of heavens and celestial paradises, and as the Lord's Prayer of Christianity hints, when the Father's will is done, this union may be possible on earth as it is in Heaven.

Though some may find this surprising, Sahaj Marg considers liberation from rebirth to be a rather low attainment in the spectrum of human possibility.

How does the idea of Grace play into all this? Do we attain by our "own effort" or by "other effort"?

Both are necessary. You cannot be given a Gift if you refuse to open your hand, and you cannot receive Grace if you refuse to open your heart. All we can do is open the door of our hearts to the Lord, our own Self, whom our ego has kicked out and who now must stand outside knocking on that closed door, closed heart, closed hand, and closed mind. We open and then we wait. Grace will be wasted if it is poured into an unprepared heart, just as milk would be wasted if it were poured into a vessel that had been used to hold gasoline. So some work, some cleaning, is necessary. We prepare our hearts to receive the Lord as we would clean our homes to receive a guest. If you have your back to the sun, Babuji used to say, all you need to do is turn around.

Yet Grace by definition can never be earned; even our tears and love and repentance cannot buy us Grace. Characteristically, Babuji clarified this ancient paradox of Work-versus-Grace with direct simplicity: "Liberation is to reveal oneself before God. Realization is when God reveals himself. Liberation can be attained by doing abhyas. Realization He may give or not; it is His prerogative."

How long does it take for one to achieve this Realization?

Realization takes an eternity and comes in an instant. It is, as Babuji hinted, a matter of Divine Grace. Though a capable Master could bring someone to the highest level in a matter of days by the force of his full transmission, such an act is forbidden, since it would destroy the physical body of the unprepared recipient. So the gradual practice or *sadhana* takes place gently and naturally for most over a period of months and years. It is like birth, which happens in an instant, but only after a time of gestation. Premature elevation in spirituality for an abhyasi is as undesirable and dangerous as is premature birth for a fetus.

But when the time is ripe, Grace descends and Realization occurs, as Lalaji said, "in less time than it takes for a tear to come from the eye." Or as Babuji once remarked, "It is only a matter of turning one's head from one side to another." Lalaji is said to have reached this moment after only seven months of practice, yet for Babuji, the sadhana continued for twenty-two years. The length of time is irrelevant, given the ultimate attainment. Time as we understand it has no relevance in the path of Realization.

Are other motives acceptable in practicing Sahaj Marg? For example, will it cure my physical illnesses? Will it help me with depression? Will it have a positive effect on my career and earning potential? I'm not sure about this "Self-Realization" stuff; I just want peace and relaxation. Is this acceptable?

It is fine to begin practice with all sorts of hopes, goals, and expectations other than the ultimate Goal just discussed. In time, as we evolve in our spiritual practice, our ideas of what is desirable will also evolve. Lesser goals drop away as we become aware of the real goal of our lives. Eventually as we advance we will develop the focus and single-pointedness of mind essential to success in this highest of all human quests, and will begin to understand why our Masters consider the things normally prized by spiritual beginners (peace of mind, wealth, health, worldly power, and so on) to be mere toys compared to the realms possible to the human spirit.

It is a fact that many who have begun Sahaj Marg practice have experienced relief from physical and emotional distress, often in ways they consider miraculous. Such testimonies abound among Sahaj Marg abhyasis, but they are rarely mentioned in public since it could generate a craze of seekers after miracles or corporeal changes which have little to do with Realization. Such blessings are given by Master to an abhyasi only if they are needed for his or her spiritual growth.

Sahaj Marg is a way of life guided by an inner spiritual purpose. A spiritual practice must give one the ability to face whatever life may present with clarity and equanimity. Thus it often happens that an abhyasi may begin Sahaj Marg only to find that all sorts of difficulties, physical and financial, begin to appear in his life! Worldly difficulties become "divine blessings" as we learn how they can help us in our spiritual goal. Lalaji used to say that three things were necessary in the making of a saint: a little financial difficulty, a little criticism, and a bit of ill health. Such difficulties remind us of the pain of desiring what is impermanent; they cure us of complacency and delusion; they spur us on toward the Real. As Lalaji said, "Afflictions are boons from God. There are many secrets in them." We have only to look to the examples of Lalaji, Babuji, and Chariji to find that even Masters are not exempt from the pains and difficulties of human life.

So while we might begin the practice of Sahaj Marg for other reasons, the sooner we come to appreciate and accept the only real Goal we have been born to realize, the less time we will waste. Meanwhile, our Master, the very embodiment and demonstration of the goal of Sahaj Marg, will patiently wait for us to cease tarrying with diversions and distractions and pursuing impermanent and useless fantasies, to have done with lesser things and seek what is Real.

How can we tell if we are progressing toward the Goal?

Chariji has said that a growing lightness of mind and spirit is the surest test of spiritual progress. Also, regardless of what mystic or cosmic experiences we may have in meditation, these signify nothing if they are not accompanied by a growing sense of harmony with our everyday world, a greater kindness and compassion for the people around us. We can be assured that we are advancing spiritually if we simply notice a dropping away of inner tension, an increase in patience and friendliness, and a growing sense of wonder and appreciation for the natural world. With just a little reflection, anyone should be able to ascertain these things for themselves, and we should need only our own experience to tell us if these qualities are developing in our lives.

No one has said that the journey is without difficulty. Along the way we experience doubts and pain, and it is not unusual for most of us to feel like quitting the practice a hundred times as we move toward this Goal. This is why a Master's help is so welcome and so necessary. He is there to guide us past the difficulties we create for ourselves, and to show us that our Goal is not far, but near.

OTHER WAYS

How does Sahaj Marg compare with other systems?

It does not. It is against etiquette to rate or compare different traditions, religions, and methods. Sahaj Marg makes no claims other than it is an effective path, simple and direct, that can be tested by anyone willing to try it. Sahaj Marg cannot testify for the efficacy of other paths.

I am a Christian. Does this mean I am converting? Should I stop going to church? Can't one be Christian or Hindu or Buddhist and also be an abhyasi? Must I give up my religion?

Taking up the practice of Sahaj Marg does not mean we are converting from one religion into another. Sahaj Marg does not require any of us to give up the external trappings of our religion. We may keep whatever is essential and necessary for our journey. Abhyasis around the world have come to Sahaj Marg from many different cultures and religions. The process of finding a connection with Divinity is internalized in Sahaj Marg, and we should not become afraid if after some time we find that desires to resort to external forms of worship or ritual begin to drop off. What is Real will remain Real, and the essence of our religion will always remain with us. As Babuji said, "Where religion ends, spirituality begins."

I am an atheist. Must I believe in God to practice? What does Sahaj Marg say about reincarnation? Is it necessary to believe in reincarnation to do this practice?

The practice of Sahaj Marg does not require a belief in God, nor does Sahaj Marg require a belief in reincarnation, since the focus of our sadhana is on this life, on the here-and-now.

In fact, Sahaj Marg has no credos, no dogma, no tenets. Sahaj Marg is experimental and experiential in its approach, and so abhyasis are asked not to simply believe what we hear or read, but to observe what we discover within; not to trust the claims of Sahaj Marg, but to test them as thoroughly as we can. Practice is something we do, not something we ponder. Until we realize for ourselves, all the claims of any spiritual practice are only secondhand information — even the testimony of the Master. Again and again, Babuji urged people who came to him to actually see for themselves: "Read and enjoy," he would say. "Do and become!"

What is the relation between Sahaj Marg and Raja Yoga?

Sahaj Marg is Raja Yoga distilled and simplified. Those acquainted with Patanjali's *Yoga Sutras* will be familiar with his classical *Ashtanga,* or Eight-Limbed, approach to Raja Yoga. The eight steps are *yama* and *niyama* (the moral and ethical limbs), *asana* (posture), *pranayama* (movement of energy through breath), *pratyahara* (withdrawal from senses), *dharana* (concentration), *dhyana* (meditation), and *samadhi* (absorption). These have often been viewed as sequential and consequential stages of development, rather like climbing the rungs of a ladder.

Whether Patanjali ever intended this is debatable, but Sahaj Marg takes a simultaneous and global approach to the practice of Raja Yoga and begins directly with dhyana or meditation, the so-called Seventh Limb. Contrary to some notions, Sahaj Marg says that meditation is simple, and points out the obvious: the only way we can ever learn to meditate is to start meditating! The tree of Raja Yoga with all its limbs can grow naturally from this seed. So the image of the ladder of steps does not fit the practice of Sahaj Marg, which is more like a sphere expanding from its center, the heart of the Light realized in meditation.

What about Karma or Bhakti or Jnana Yoga?

Though Sahaj Marg is usually presented as a refinement of Raja Yoga, it must be understood as a synthesis of the other primary yogas as well. As outlined in the Bhagavad Gita, the four essential yogas are Karma Yoga (work and service), Jnana Yoga (discrimination and wisdom), Bhakti Yoga (supreme and dissolving adoration, love, and devotion), and Raja Yoga (the so-called "yoga of the king," as it involves the mind or "king" of all senses and the direct, experiential perception of the Absolute). Experience proves that the four yogas are not rigidly exclusive, but that after a certain level they intersect and blend, and ultimately arrive at a state where all paths end and such distinctions are of no consequence.

What about Hatha or Vinyasa Yoga?

Currently popular, Vinyasa is one the many schools of Hatha Yoga, which is by far the most well-known form of yoga in the West. Hatha Yoga focuses on breath and body postures or asanas. It is fine for physical well-being, but for approaching the spiritual depths, across the centuries, the great yogins have considered Raja Yoga as the most direct path.

It is only natural for the Sahaj Marg abhyasi to respect and care for his or her body, to get proper rest and nourishment and exercise. But we should not become obsessed or fixated on the body, which, after all, is not permanent. No matter how flexible it becomes or what remarkable feats it can be trained to accomplish, the body is finally fated to die and drop away. For sensible physical exercise, an abhyasi may do whatever is helpful — walking, jogging, swimming, or whatever — as long as these activities do not take time from the spiritual practice. Doing Tai Chi or Hatha Yoga for the purpose of physical well-being may be harmless, but since these practices often go beyond simple exercise, the abhyasi should always be cautious about mixing energies. "When in doubt," as Master likes to say, "don't."

What about Nada or Taraka Yoga, Kriya Yoga, and Tantric or Kundalini Yoga?

There are dozens of yogas in the East and the West, and if you feel attracted to these forms, you should go to a proper teacher of that tradition. Some abhyasis do have experience of the inner sound or *shabda* of nada-yoga, the various light-visions (*lakshya*) common to taraka-yoga. Though *kundalini* may be awakened in Sahaj Marg practice if Master deems this to be necessary for an abhyasi's appointed work, kundalini as such involves power and has nothing to do with spiritual realization.

I am already practicing some meditation; why can't I just do both Sahaj Marg and another practice?

Just as it is unwise to mix and take different prescriptions from two or three doctors, so it is dangerous to mix spiritual practices. Such a question might suggest a confused, restless, or even greedy attitude. Only one boat is required to cross a river; straddling two usually results in capsizing, not arriving. Dabbling and flirting among spiritual paths may be like drilling one well only a little way, then giving up because the work is hard and the water doesn't come, then moving to another spot and drilling again. Such work is not only wasteful, but fruitless, for all we end up with is a dozen or a thousand shallow holes. Better to gather all that scattered effort and sink a single deep well — for all we need is but one well that goes all the way and we can then draw from an entire reservoir.

In short, once you have shopped around among various traditions, it may be wise to choose one method and follow it wholeheartedly — with *ekagrata*, the clear and single-pointed focus deemed essential for spiritual practice. Entrants to any spiritual path should take up that practice fully and purely. This is why we are advised to put our former practices on hold while we are giving Sahaj Marg a test.

How does the Master compare with Masters in other traditions?

Speaking of when he was an abhyasi under Babuji, Chariji once said, "I never compared my Master to other Masters. I only compared myself to my Master." This says much in few words.

Along these lines, Babuji recorded that Lalaji gave him certain directions to be observed during *bhandara* (spiritual gatherings), one of which is: "There should be no differentiation between the gurus or disciples of other institutions and one's own." These words also invite deep contemplation.

One last point: Eager disciples of various traditions often squabble and dispute about the superiority of their path over all others, or the primacy of their guru above all others, but this is not the case among genuine and true Masters, who must smile at such childish behavior among the devotees of supposedly competing camps. One of the first things we learn in associating with our Master is that at the higher levels, all beings work in harmony, and that no incorporeal being or human guru, hidden or revealed, works without Nature's permission. The Masters form a harmony across time and space and also across all traditions, taking the work that is appointed to them by Nature. Only their less mature disciples, who do not yet see the grandness of Nature's whole panorama, foolishly argue for this guru or that guru as the "greatest."

Then Sahaj Marg is not the "only way" to God Realization?

Sahaj Marg rejects the notion that there is "one true way" for every person everywhere. Just as a mother might prepare a dish in different ways to please her different children, so has God created many paths to suit the needs of Her children in their particular situations. The paths we choose at given times in our lives are thus more a matter of suitability or even our karmic destiny. The ancient Vedic principle applies here: "Paths are many; Truth is one."

And yet there is another level of understanding (see *invertendo*) regarding this question of paths. Babuji once said, "There is only one way to attain God. Had there been several paths, even thieves would have reached Him by a secret path." The truth is, no matter what tradition or method we adopt, in essence there is only one way to realize God.

Though the surface instances vary, all human beings are essentially born in the same way, and all die in the same way. Just so, regardless of our language or culture or belief system, we all sleep, dream, and awaken in the same way. And we all enter the *turiya*, the "fourth consciousness," in the same way — that is, we simply drop our delusions and awaken to Reality. How many ways are there to drop a burning ember from our hands? As the ancient sages used to say, "The paths to Hell are many; but to God there is only one Path." In that path to God, no matter what external words, rituals, or techniques are used, the inner process for all is single, eternal, and universal.

Finally, the spiritually mature individual recognizes the beauty and validity of other paths, but he or she is not fickle-minded and does not confuse this appreciation with an inability to commit to a given practice. Generally speaking, regardless of our chosen path, three qualities are essential for all spiritual travelers: Tolerance or appreciation of all paths is, according to Sahaj Marg, the beginning, not the end, of spirituality. *Viveka* (insight or discrimination) is a second prerequisite. Intense longing (*mumuksha*) is the third.

I already have a Guru. May I still practice the method of Sahaj Marg? Must I give my old Master up? I feel grateful to him/her.

If people find their practice or current guru to be satisfactory, Chariji encourages them to follow that path to its furthest reach. By the same token, if someone feels that he or she can receive no further benefit from a practice or guru, then it is his or her right and duty to try to find a more effective path. Chariji has said, "But please, only one Marg at a time!"

To this we might add, "Please, one Master at a time." Ultimately the Way and the Guru are inseparable, for as it has been said, "A teacher points the Way; the Guru is the Way." Thus we may have many teachers, but we can have only one Guru, once we really understand the role of the Guru in the life of a disciple. Trying to serve two masters is a disservice not only to our former guru, but to ourselves as well.

In another way, to the degree that a former guru has taught and assisted us, none of us ever has to give up such benefit. We may be lucky enough to have learned from many wise teachers or *upa-gurus* (secondary gurus), and should always feel gratitude and respect for them. When we graduate out of high school into college, it is not an act of betrayal to our high school teachers, but a normal process of growth and expansion.

True gurus exist to serve us, not the other way around. Babuji has written: "I hold it to be the birthright of every man to break off from his Guru if he finds he has made a wrong selection or had misjudged that Guru's capacity or worth. He is also free to seek another Guru if at any stage he finds that his Guru has not the capacity to take him beyond that which he has already acquired. On the other hand, a conscientious Guru must himself, under the circumstances, direct his disciple to seek another more advanced and better qualified, so that the disciple may not in any way suffer progress. This is the sacred duty of a true and selfless Guru. If, however, permission to break off, sought for by the disciple, is denied by the Guru on account of his selfish motives, the disciple is at liberty to break off from him at once and seek another. No moral or religious law ever forbids him from doing so."

I regret having wasted so much time in other practices.

Please understand that there is no need for regret, because the time was not wasted. We all need to go through various experiences before we are consciously introduced to the one destined to be our Master. It is probable that we have been connected with our Master long before we actually meet him, perhaps even over a period of many lives. Only when the time is right can our Master make himself known, but until that time, his influence and grace have been working even though we did not or could not recognize it as such. Later, we may come to see that there are no accidents, only Divine plans.

The revealing of the Master is actually the culmination of a long period of gestation and hidden work. This work comes in the form of experiences of all kinds, from tragedy and loss, to growth and learning within a variety of religious traditions, to simple and direct insights given by Divine Grace. When the soil is prepared and nourished, the seed will sprout and break through into the sunlight, and that moment can come only because it has gone through a time of development in the dark underground. So it is with the Divine in our hearts and lives.

What does Sahaj Marg say about Jesus? I think Jesus is the only Way. Jesus said, "For one is your master, even Christ." (Mt. 23.10)

As we have already said, if you feel that Christ or anyone else is your Master, you should stay with Him.

It is the view of Sahaj Marg, however, that representatives of God are born in different times and places to give people an approach to the Divine that is suitable to their current situation and condition. Masters appear in ordinary human form, go through the troubles all of us must endure, and then return to the Source that sent them forth. There are reasons why the Divine must take on various human forms to appear as Masters to different cultures and races and times, and Christ Himself gave a hint along these lines when He said: "As long as I am in the world, I am the light of the world." (John 9.5) When Jesus spoke of the reincarnation or return of the Christ — "For as the lightening cometh out of the east and shineth even unto the west; so shall also the coming of the Son of man be," (Mt. 24.27) — He added: "Therefore be ye also ready, for in such an hour as ye think not the Son of man cometh." (Mt. 24.44 and Luke 12.40) Will we be ready to recognize the Master when He appears before us? The appearance of our Master may not be during an apocalypse: all Jesus says is that the Master will appear before us unexpectedly, perhaps in a form we never anticipated.

Chariji loves to tell the following story. It is a story about a group of very religious Brahmins begging for a visit from Lord Krishna, who was to them what Christ is to others: the only true full incarnation of God. Lord Krishna spoke and told the Brahmins that He had heard their prayers and would come have supper with them at midnight. Overjoyed, the Brahmins performed all the necessary ablutions and said the proper mantras, and under a *pandal* or canopy in a holy grove laid out a wonderful repast. Then they waited. Suddenly at midnight a wild pig burst out of the underbrush and began rooting and snouting through the food they had laid out for their Lord. Horrified that an unclean animal was polluting the Lord's supper, they began to beat the pig and drive it away. A strange thing happened, as the story goes: Every time they hit the pig, they felt the blows on their own bodies as well! Finally they drove the pig squealing back into the forest, but the food was ruined and Krishna never appeared. The next morning, the Brahmins glumly performed their rites and then demanded that Krishna explain why He had broken His promise to come and have supper with them. This time Lord Krishna did appear before the Brahmins. "I did come," he told them, "but obviously not in the form you were expecting!" Then He turned and the Brahmins received a second shock. Their Lord's back was covered with the stripes and bruises they'd given to that pig!

Buddhist and Hindu scriptures also agree that spiritual Masters appear in every generation to assist humanity and do the work of nature. Some are known, but many choose to remain hidden. Of those who are known, some become *jagat-gurus*, or world-teachers, and are worshipped for many centuries. If their teachings are deep enough, and true enough, eventually they may crystallize into a scripture and produce a religion. All religions begin with the realization of a single individual, and the original experience of its founder remains the bedrock of each religion. Whether that founder is Christ, Buddha, Rama, Krishna, Mohammed, or someone else, this standard holds true, and to the degree that the founder's followers can partake of that experience themselves, their religion continues to be valid and transformative rather than degenerating into a set of mechanical rituals or a dry body of social obligations.

Sahaj Marg respects the Masters of all religions. This brief book is not the place to go into depth about the harmony of the words of Christ and the practice of Sahaj Marg, but a deep parallel study of the Gospels and the works of Sahaj Marg Masters might dispel apparent or superficial conflicts. You may bring your conflicts directly to Chariji, or to a knowledgeable brother or sister, if you wish, but your practice itself will provide the ultimate verification. After some time, you will know the truth directly for yourself. As Jesus said, "The kingdom of God is within." Just so, Sahaj Marg advises us only to meditate and look within our own heart. The definition, the description, and the destination of meditation was never expressed so well as in Psalms 46.10: "Be still and know that I am God."

BEGINNING SAHAJ MARG

How do I begin Sahaj Marg? What exactly is to be done?

The first step is to meet with a preceptor. (For names and addresses of the preceptors nearest you, please contact one of the centers listed at the end of this book.) You should be given a minimum of three individual sittings from a preceptor before attending group meditation. Ideally, these sittings should occur over two or three days. The second sitting should come within twenty-four hours of the first.

What is a "sitting"? What precisely is done during the introductory sittings?

The term "sitting" is used in Sahaj Marg to describe a meditation in which the Master or a preceptor meditates in the presence of a group or with an individual to clean the subtle body and transmit prana. This is normally done while sitting face to face — or more precisely, heart to heart. The introductory sittings are devoted mostly to cleaning the system of the beginner. Subtle obstacles are removed and the way is prepared for open-hearted meditation.

It should be noted that three introductory sittings are the *minimum*. Sahaj Marg does not treat human beings as if they were assembly-line products, and recognizes that the condition and capacity of each individual is unique. So you should not be concerned if the preceptor requests more sittings — it does not mean that your condition is exceptionally gross or, on the other hand, that your capacity is especially great. What it means is that the preceptor wants to give you as firm a beginning as possible, and if you are willing, he or she would like to give you more than the bare minimum of sittings. Babuji once gave twenty-two sittings to a person beginning the practice.

Why must I contact a preceptor for introductory sittings? Why can't I just learn the method and practice Sahaj Marg on my own?

Actually, you could — but why would you want to? It is a fact that in less than five minutes, almost anyone could pick up the simple techniques of Sahaj Marg — the placing of Divine light in the heart, the evening cleaning, the bedtime prayer, and so on. But simply because the methods of Sahaj Marg have never been kept secret (all of them are described in this book, for example), we should not misunderstand this as implying that they are given for us to privately experiment with them in an idiosyncratic, cavalier, or maverick manner.

Please consider why you are asking such a question in the first place. We may feel hesitant to fully commit ourselves to a practice with other people, even on a trial basis. Many of us are reluctant because we think that we may be expected to join a group or organization (see the section titled "Satsangh"). Please understand that receiving introductory sittings from a preceptor obliges no one to become a member of any group or organization.

The preceptor (along with other abhyasis) is simply a person who is available to serve you and help you with your practice. It is the norm, not the exception, that beginners will make mistakes in Sahaj Marg practice, simple as it seems, which can easily be corrected by an attentive preceptor, but which otherwise can develop into difficult problems — like picking up bad habits as a beginning golfer, which are easy to detect and correct when they first develop, but hard to remedy once they have become ingrained. You might consider the preceptor in the same way you think of a coach or a personal trainer in the physical realm. Even long after the beginning stage, many questions and situations arise in our individual practice that are not dealt with in books, and for these, the personal assistance of a preceptor can be invaluable.

Finally, we should recognize that opening our hearts to Divine transmission *is* the method of Sahaj Marg, as the response to the previous question suggests. Indeed, without transmission, we are not practicing Sahaj Marg at all, but something else of our own invention. Transmission is central to Sahaj Marg practice; it is the way we can be connected directly with the Source. Without such a connection, we can copy the techniques of the meditation and try to practice them on our own, but this is rather like trying to compose a program on the keyboard of a computer that is not plugged in to the power source. Such an approach could be likened to sitting in a sailboat inside a boathouse - though we could put up all kinds of sails and practice any number of techniques, without the wind of Divine transmission, such efforts can bring little or no real change in our position. Again, it would be like learning how to waltz from an instruction-book, and going through the motions in a silent, empty room. But surely a dance is more than a mere series of technical steps. The music that is Divine Transmission, the dancing partner that is the Master, and all the other dancers in the ballroom that are our brothers and sisters, certainly these make the waltz come alive with joy and magic and beauty.

In short, you cannot begin the practice of Sahaj Marg by merely imitating the techniques you read in this book. Sahaj Marg does not exist without a living connection with All, which is precipitated and nourished in our hearts by the transmission of the Master.

What qualifications or requirements are necessary for one to begin the practice of Sahaj Marg?

Anyone who is at least eighteen years old and who is willing to make a sincere commitment to try the practice for three to six months may begin.

Why must one be at least eighteen years of age to begin practice?

Sahaj Marg recognizes the fact that all humans must grow and develop in a natural way at a natural pace. As we mature, we first learn to crawl, then walk, then talk, then read, and so on. Just so, with spirituality, children should be allowed to grow and play and develop in a natural way. They must not be forced into meditation before they have the maturity to understand something of what they are getting into, and can make an independent decision for themselves, apart from the pressures of parents or peers. Granted, some individuals mature early, and others seem to never mature, but the age of eighteen has been selected as an arbitrary time when most of us are first able to consider choosing a spiritual path. Master sometimes allows individuals to begin sadhana before they turn eighteen, but this is rather rare.

Are any fees or donations required for spiritual training under Sahaj Marg?

No. How can you be charged for having restored to you that which has always been yours? Sahaj Marg holds that spirituality cannot be sold any more than the sky can be sold, for no one owns it.

I have too many bad habits to start a spiritual practice at this time. Much as I might like to, I'm afraid that I cannot leave my vices.

Sahaj Marg is not for perfect people, but for those who are willing to become perfect. We all have vices which may seem horrible and special to us, but which are almost always quite commonplace. These weaknesses, inclinations, or compulsions do not disqualify us; in fact, they are the very reasons to take up a spiritual practice. In Sahaj Marg, we do not battle directly with our desires — such an attack only makes the desires more strong, as anyone who has ever made a New Year's resolution will know. Rather than focus on our faults, in Sahaj Marg we simply make progress in the good and allow habits to drop away by themselves. There is no force, no rush. The process is quite natural and happens when the time is ripe.

Sometimes the *samskaras* (the subtle impressions that give rise to habits) are removed very quickly, and change is almost effortless. At other times, the abhyasi must work again and again to manifest externally the internal cleaning that has been given by the Master. As Master says, some samskaras are removed only with the abhyasi's cooperation in the form of consistent effort, with perhaps many failures, before the result becomes an abiding condition. The difficulties are sometimes left in place by the Master to help the abhyasi develop character. In other instances, habits that once seemed impossible to escape can be cleared in a way that seems truly miraculous. Whatever is necessary for an abhyasi's progress will be given.

Once a group of men came to Babuji and said, "Sir, we admire your system very much, but we cannot start." Babuji asked them why not. These fellows were unusual in that they were not shamed and secretive, but came right out and told Babuji about their shortcomings as a way of explaining why they felt themselves to be unsuitable candidates for spiritual practice. "Sir," they concluded flatly, "we cannot leave our vices."

Babuji laughed. "I am telling you," he replied, "do not worry about leaving your vices. They will leave you!"

I think I might like to give the system a try, but at this point I cannot promise that I will stay with it forever. Is this acceptable?

Of course. This is essentially what Babuji meant when he used to say that the only requirement to begin Sahaj Marg is *willingness*. Much is contained in that single word, for the proper beginning is one made not just from the level of the emotions, which may fluctuate with every change of circumstance, but also from the deeper level of the will. For this level to remain engaged, we must remember the purpose and destination of our lives. Like a sailor holding a true course, it is this one-pointedness of mind that will carry us through the cross-winds of desire amidst the clamorous attractions we see all around us, and also through those doldrums, momentary despairs, or simply the lack of interest that inevitably beset every spiritual voyager from time to time.

Why are we asked to devote three to six months to test the practice of Sahaj Marg?

A reasonable length of time is necessary to give the results of the practice time to manifest. This is true not just with Sahaj Marg, but with any spiritual practice. The time period of three to six months is somewhat arbitrary, in that often these changes can be felt much sooner, and sometimes a greater amount of time may be necessary, particularly as the work advances and grows more and more subtle.

How exactly are we supposed to tell if the practice is working? What changes should we expect during this trial period?

As mentioned earlier, Master has said that the surest test of the effectiveness of a spiritual practice is a growing sense of lightness. Now this sense of lightness is by definition a subjective condition. It might be compared to a daughter asking her mother about the experience of falling in love. "How will I know when I have fallen in love?" she might ask her mother. And the mother will smile and say, "Don't worry. You'll know."

Just so, though this sense of spiritual lightness may difficult to describe, it is one that can be easily recognized when it is experienced. Even after a short time of practice, many abhyasis often report a dropping away of complexities, a sense of peace, a heightened intuitive ability, a sense of focus and direction.

When Reality is perceived, the response is awe and gratitude. One test for the clarity of our contact with the Real is whether we experience a sense of abiding gratitude as a kind of background to the other emotions that pass by — or its reverse, resentment and bitterness. The one is light, clear, open and soft; the other — resentment — is dark, smoky, closed, and hard.

But the most simple and honest way to describe how we have found our chosen path is that after some time, it simply feels right. We come to feel that for us, no matter that we may continue to doubt and struggle and argue, Sahaj Marg has become "the path with a heart."

But understand that whatever feelings arise, whether they are agreeable to us or not, all such conditions will change and pass on. In our spiritual *yatra* or journey toward the Ultimate, peace will come and go, pain will arrive and depart, until we at last come into what Babuji has described as the unchanging condition, the non-bliss blissfulness, the peace beyond peace.

Finally, regarding expectations, however, a word of caution: it is almost a rule of spiritual practice that one of the first experiences that comes along is the realization that our expectations are in themselves hindrances and obstacles (as the second line of the Mission prayer suggests) and this realization usually comes when our hidden expectations are revealed precisely because they are *not* met! We may expect a guru to look and act in a certain way, and the genuine guru will often disappoint and frustrate those expectations. So it is best to simply do the practice and observe whatever arises, including our own expectations. For what we expect to happen will condition (and therefore limit) what actually does happen. This is a truth with any spiritual practice.

Sooner or later, the time for action comes. This, finally, is the only way we can satisfy our own questioning. Do, and see for yourself.

What are the suggested guidelines for the trial period?

The following suggestions may be considered:

1. *Do the practice for a reasonable length of time to allow the subtle changes to begin to flower.* Even for physical training, we could hardly expect to see results from only one or two workouts in a gymnasium. Three to six months should suffice as a minimum provisional commitment to any new method of spiritual training. There are many terrains in the geography of the inner world, and we should not be surprised or discouraged when we hit dry places and valleys, just as we should not get elated by the first view from the mountains.

2. *Do the practice fully, as it is meant to be done.* To extend the metaphor of working in a gymnasium, we could hardly expect to see any results even after the three or six months if we had only worked out a few times each month. In Sahaj Marg, this means doing

43

the daily practice, attending satsangh once a week, getting at least two individual sittings from a preceptor each month, writing in our spiritual diary, reading, and so on.

3. *Do the practice without adding to it and without altering it.* We can hardly evaluate the results of one practice if it is mixed into an eclectic stew of other practices. When we have practiced Sahaj Marg honestly, singly, and thoroughly for three to six months, then if we find it does not suit us, our former practices will always be there for us to take up again. But we must be willing to put them "on hold" while we are testing a new practice.

A century ago Swami Vivekananda likened the enthusiasms of Americans to a fire of straw — "quickly ignited, but quickly extinguished." Only when the novelty of the practice and the initial "honeymoon phase" is gone does the work begin in earnest. Unfortunately, this is when many leave the practice, and move on to something else or drop the effort altogether. Such a pattern has been aptly described as an "addiction to attraction," whereby people either fear commitment or become fixated with novelty, wishing to sample a bit of everything in love or life or spirituality without diving deeply. We must be more mature than this, and see how limiting the restless gravitation toward novelty can be and the opportunities it may deny. Then, though we may appreciate other ways, still we can dive deeply in the tradition we have chosen — or as some say, has been chosen for us. The Source of all paths may remain illusory as long as we keep skittering from surface to surface, but may be perceived when the depths are sounded. Only then can true

appreciation for all paths begin to develop. So, Master says:
"Dive deep!"

I have noticed that many of those who begin Sahaj Marg in the West do not even stick with it for the initial three months. Why do they leave?

This question could have as many answers as the number of individuals who begin the practice but for some reason, drop off — indeed, often before completing even the trial period they agreed to observe. It is not fair to broadbrush all those who make such aborted beginnings as fickle-minded or flaky. In fact, preceptors usually feel that they are the ones who have failed in such cases, not the individuals who came to them for instruction and transmission.

Traditionally, those who wished to learn from a guru had to pass certain tests before they would be accepted for instruction. The guru would ignore the aspiring disciple or even attempt to drive him away. Stories of severe testing of an applicant's seriousness of purpose by the guru abound in dharmic literature. Bodhidharma is said to have accepted the disciple who was to become the Second Patriarch only after the fellow got his attention by cutting off his own right arm and presenting it as evidence to his Master that he was indeed serious about his own evolution. This used to be symbolically represented in the Zen Buddhist tradition, where candidates were expected to wait outside the monastery walls for days, knocking and begging to be admitted — but it also was more than symbolic. Garbage would be dumped on these poor souls and insults hurled at them; they might even get beaten, and be ordered to leave. Finally, those who could not be driven away would be admitted.

There are no such traditional dramas or external tests of the applicant in Sahaj Marg. Beginning the practice of Sahaj Marg is very easy. It is democratic and open to all, regardless of creed, gender, maturity, education, financial situation, race, or religion. All anyone has to do is profess a willingness to begin and take three introductory sittings from a preceptor. Nonetheless, in Sahaj Marg the testing of the applicant's sincerity and fortitude is just as real as in the old traditions, and it comes just as quickly — only here, the one who does the testing is also the one who is being tested, namely, the applicant himself.

One wishes the best for those who decide that Sahaj Marg does not suit them after they have given the system a sincere effort for three to six months. Indeed, as already mentioned, Sahaj Marg does not hold the view that everyone must follow the same spiritual path; Sahaj Marg simply says follow the path you choose wholeheartedly. It is regrettable when a practice is rejected before it has been properly tested. We may have carelessly thrown away a jewel without even knowing we once held it in our hand.

Chariji once asked Babuji why he could not use his powers as a Master to make people stay with the practice, because even if they couldn't recognize the fact, this was what they needed more than anything else in life. Babuji replied, "Yes, it could be done, but it is not allowed. Man is not an animal that he can be tied up." No matter how much God may yearn for reunion with his children, apparently He will never force anyone to come to Him. We must each come of our own will. And each day we stay, it is because of our will, until the day finally comes when God's will and our will are one.

In human existence, no quest is more challenging than the quest to master one's own self and to realize God within. Indeed, this inner adventure is so daunting that few will even begin in earnest, and of these even fewer will remain to finish. Lord Krishna, speaking as God, put it this way: "Among thousands of men, perhaps one strives for perfection; among thousands who strive, perhaps one knows me in truth." (*Bhagavad Gita* 7.2)

For this reason the ancients used to say that no one should begin the practice of yoga unless he or she has the same intensity of purpose and singleness of will that a person whose hair has caught fire will use in putting that fire out. Everything else — family, career, food — is eclipsed in the bright fire of that *mumuksha,* or desire for liberation. Few of us have that degree of yearning for Realization, but if such restlessness begins to develop in our practice, we may count ourselves blessed, for Realization will follow such a pure intention as the light follows the rising sun.

THE MASTER

What does the term "Master" mean in Sahaj Marg?

In casual usage, "Master" is merely the appellation used by most abhyasis in referring to the gurus of the Sahaj Marg lineage, and in particular, to the living Representative. Truly speaking, however, the external Master or Guru can be described as the reflection of our own inner Teacher. This is true not only for Masters of Sahaj Marg, but for the Masters of all the great traditions. Along these lines, the words of Tibetan Lama Sogyal Rinpoche can hardly be improved upon: "The master whose human shape and human voice we come to love with a love deeper than any other in our lives is none other than the external manifestation of the mystery of our own inner truth. What else could explain why we feel so strongly connected to him?"

Officially within Shri Ram Chandra Mission (SRCM), the Master is the spiritual Representative nominated by his Master, who carries on the spiritual duties as guided and instructed by his Master. As such, there is only one living Master at a time, who also accepts the responsibilities of President of SRCM.

But Chariji has often explained that the use of the word "master" in Sahaj Marg has nothing to do with some external hierarchical relationship, in which one person acts like a boss whose every order must be obeyed, and all others are mere lowly slaves. In fact, Sahaj Marg Masters rarely give direct orders to others, and then only to advanced abhyasis, or when absolutely necessary. Instead, they tend to give subtle hints or general suggestions. Masters, as Babuji always insisted, come not to rule, but only to serve. The most striking characteristic of our Masters are their utter ordinariness, their lack of self-consciousness, their playfulness, and their genuine humility.

For example, Chariji has answered the question "Who is the Master?" in many different ways, depending on how he feels, and on who is asking, and why, and when, and where.

He has replied: "A Master is not who you think he is."

Or: "I would say that the Master is nobody."

Or: "The Master is someone very much like you!"

The hint here is that the Master is not a riddle to be solved or a definition to be settled and set away, but is a mystery best approached with wonder. It is a mystery in which the Master is both a human being and yet not a human being, but something beyond, as Babuji hinted:

"I started practice at the age of twenty-one when I did not know what is surrender and so I never tried for that. To me my Master was all and all, because I got such a Master. If there was any surrender on my part unconsciously, it was to the Master alone. Really speaking, the frame of the Master is not God, but what is behind it is Divinity. So I submitted to that Divinity and not the physical being. If you invite into your view the whole frame of the Master, the Divinity will lag behind. (It was for me alone. I never say for others to do it.) So it was not submission to the Master but to the Real Being. But now my own experience wants that our associates may reap the benefit of my experiences."

So the "Master" may be viewed as either an incarnated human being or as Being itself, prior to and beyond any incarnation. But really the Master must be seen as both. The "frame of the Master" and the "Divinity behind it" cannot be separated, for just as we cannot separate water from the abstract concept of wetness, so we cannot divide the temporal Master from the eternal Divinity the Master embodies.

Two more things can be said. Chariji has explained that in Sahaj Marg, the word "master" can refer to a person who has mastered himself or herself. Most of us will admit that this is no common feat. As already suggested, it is this mastery over self, not mastery over others, that makes one a true master. Secondly, in the living tradition of Sahaj Marg, a Master is one who has the ability to transmit from the center of his own existence to the center of another's existence, who can thus awaken and nurture the Master in others. In short, a Master is able to create not just disciples, but others like himself, that is, another Master. But this work can be done only if a fit disciple appears and is willing to undergo the work and fulfill his own part of the bargain. Sadly, few have the faith and courage to accept this reality, for as Babuji used to say, "Rare to find a Master of caliber, but even more rare to find a disciple of caliber!"

How does one recognize a Master of caliber?

In sum, by becoming a disciple of caliber.

Chariji has said that if we have one Goal, the highest goal in mind, it is easy to find guidance, and Babuji has attested that a sincere prayer will bring the guru to our door!

Babuji goes into some detail to help us in our search for a genuine and capable Master: "It is very difficult to find such a person, but they are there, no doubt, in this world. I will tell you an easy method of finding them out. If you sit beside such a person, never mind be he a *sannyasi* (renunciate) or *grihastha* (householder), calmness, the nature of self, will remain predominant and you will be care-free for the time being. You will be in touch with the Real thing so long as you are with him. The effect is automatic, even if he does not exert himself.

"If you really want to search for such a person, what you have to do is only to look to your own heart and note the condition of your mind. It becomes comparatively calm and quiet, and the different ideas that have been haunting your mind and troubling you all the time are away so long as you are with him.

"But one thing is to be clearly borne in mind, that mind should not in any way be taxed and there should be no heaviness. Because this effect (keeping off the ideas and bringing the mind to a stand-still) can be brought off also by those who have mastered the baser science of hypnotism. The difference between the two is that in the latter case heaviness, exhaustion, and dullness of mind and physique will be felt, while in the former case the person will feel lightness and at the same time calmness prevailing all over. It is possible that you may not be able to judge it at first glance, but constant company with the person will surely offer you clear hints and indications in this respect."

51

What is the role of the Master?

As indicated, the Master's duty is to awaken and nurture the Divine in all who seek such assistance, and thus fulfill his pledge to his own Master. The Master in Sahaj Marg takes complete responsibility for the abhyasi's total well-being, but only when the abhyasi allows this through intelligent surrender to Divine will. What is meant by "intelligent surrender" is not that we surrender our intelligence, but that we surrender *because of* our intelligence.

I feel that the idea of a Master somehow comes between me and God. Why must we have a Master? Can't everyone go to God directly, without any intermediary?

Babuji wrote, "God is the real Guru or Master and we get Light from Him alone. But as it is extremely difficult for a man of ordinary talents to draw inspiration from God directly, we seek the help of one of our fellow beings who has established his connection with the Almighty. It is quite evident that if a man comes out as a guru or master he has usurped the position really due to God and as such it is nothing but mere blasphemy. [The guru] must, therefore, treat himself as the humblest servant of God, serving humanity in the name of the great Master."

It is true that we can indeed go to the Source directly, without any assistance from a fellow human being, and we are welcome to try whenever we like. But we may come to understand why such a feat is very rare in the long history of the spiritual traditions of the world, and why most agree on the desirability, indeed the necessity, for a Realized Master in human form to assist most seekers in finding their way Home. If we honestly examine the sources of our desire to "go it alone," we may find the very thing that stands between ourselves and reality — namely, the subtle pride in accomplishment and the fear of surrender that are the signatures of ego. It is this ego, not the Master, that "comes between me and God."

But I still do not like the idea of having to depend on some external authority figure and giving them power over me.

This question betrays a fundamental misunderstanding of the guru-disciple relationship, which is one of mutual love and respect. A true guru exercises no more authority over a student than a grandfather does with a grandchild. In this kind of love, such bristling over authority does not arise in disciples any more than it would among grandchildren.

And yet the Guru is more than a loving grandparent. If we truly realized how difficult the path to Reality before us actually is, how fraught with a thousand subtle traps, wrong turns, dead ends, false realizations, self-deceit, and outright delusion, we would rush to find a competent guide! Of course, as long as we are happy to remain in the familiar neighborhood of the social religion we were born into by an accident of geography, we need no Guru — we can easily make do with the local priests or rabbis or mullahs, or with our own little lights, for that matter. But if we hope to climb the Himalayas of human possibility, it is a wise idea to find a sherpa! If you wish to know the way, says the old proverb, ask the one who goes up and down upon it.

If you prefer, think of the Master as a spiritual trainer or coach, and try to accept the services he offers in the way you might accept the services, for instance, of a dance instructor. It would be difficult to learn to waltz if we only read manuals about waltzing and never listen to waltz music or see the dance performed. Much simpler and faster to find a dancing master, who can show us in a few steps what we could never learn even from years of reading. The Master embodies the Goal, just as a dancer embodies the dance — and how can we imagine a dance apart from a dancer?

Finally, as for the reluctance to "give another person power over us," do we not already do this almost daily? When we fly in an airplane, we trust our very lives to the pilot, airplane mechanics, air traffic controllers, and others we have never met. We completely surrender ourselves to the care of surgeons when necessary. The same life-and-death trust occurs every time we even drive a car — we must trust each oncoming driver to be skillful and stay in his own lane. Other examples of the necessity of provisional but complete trust are everywhere, from going to barbers to aerobics instructors. Our entire existence is one of interdependence, and if we honestly look at all the aspects of our material life, we would see that there are really no areas in which we can claim to wield complete autonomy or independent determination. So why must we insist on independence in our spiritual journey?

But what about all the abuses of unscrupulous gurus?

Sadly, it is true that charlatans or sincere psychotics often attract large followings who honestly consider them to be true gurus. This is as true today as it has been for centuries; it is part of the Dance. The existence of failed or counterfeit gurus does not imply that the genuine article isn't out there somewhere for these tragic figures to imitate, since travesties are impossible without the established reality of an original. That authentic Rembrandts exist is not negated by the forged copies that surface; indeed, his mastery is confirmed by the counterfeits — for what fool would try to pass off a forged copy of something that was of no value, or never existed in reality? It would be like making counterfeits of pennies or of 25-dollar bills. Gloating over false teachers and tragically deluded cults may be comforting for us, since it allows us to remain in our cynical easy-chairs and do nothing about our own spiritual journeys, but is a bit too facile to dismiss the possibility that living gurus exist based on the behavior of a few sensationalized *poseurs*. As someone said, it is like refusing to receive money because there have been some forged notes floating about somewhere.

If I am uncomfortable and shy about the idea of accepting someone as my Master, can I still do the practice of Sahaj Marg?

Absolutely. In fact, Chariji himself practiced Sahaj Marg for months before he even found out that there was a Guru behind the system, and only later did he actually meet Babuji face to face. Chariji has said that no one can be expected to love someone he has never met, much less accept that person as his Master. So when we first begin the practice, no one is expected to do this; in fact, no abhyasi is asked at any time to accept Chariji or anyone else as his or her Master. The relationship with a Master is a very personal matter and develops at first just like any other human relationship. It usually requires time to deepen from polite respect, to friendship, and perhaps ultimately to love, awe, and wonder.

Traditions from all over the world and across hundreds of centuries agree: Knowing a true Guru is the greatest delight and the most fortunate experience that can come to a human being. Many abhyasis come to understand that there exists no experience more wonderful and endlessly fascinating than to enter into the field of a worthy Guru. It is a relationship which gradually expands to fill the entire universe, and is a mystery which embraces all other possible human relationships — mother and infant, father and son, friend and companion, mentor and student, lover and beloved.

But no one has to accept this to practice Sahaj Marg.

How is a Master chosen?

It is said that the Grand Masters select the successor to the present Master. For example, Lalaji selected Chariji as Babuji's successor. Similarly, Babuji might select Chariji's successor. This also would introduce another and most important element of impartiality and deservingness to this system of Spiritual Inheritance. Of course, the mysteries of succession are finally the responsibility of the Masters, and are outside the scope of the work of an abhyasi — even, one might add, that abhyasi determined to become the successor to his Master!

Is Master an ordinary human being, or is He Divine? Can a Master make mistakes? Does he ever change his mind? Is the Master growing and changing like the rest of us?

Master is both human and divine, as are we all. He is no less human than you or I, and he is no more Divine than you or I. As an analogy, we might think of water. Whether it is in the form of a vast ocean, or a great cascade like Niagara Falls, or a small pond, or even a fetid sewer, the water is always the same. A Master might be likened to an ocean where we might be a pond, or (alas!) perhaps a sewer. But the water, even if it contains dirt and filth, is still water. All that is required is cleaning and purifying. Just so, our essential nature is and has always been Divine, nothing needs to be added to the Original Divine Essence. A Master merely expresses greater purity and amplitude of this Essence than most beings.

Yes, a Master can make a mistake. In fact, Babuji used to joke that a Master was greater than God, because a Master could make mistakes, whereas God cannot! (This might also be one explanation for Babuji's mysterious remark, "God is limited, but Master is unlimited.") Like all human beings a Master changes his mind, learns new things, grows, and evolves. Asked if he is still changing and growing, Chariji looked surprised that the question would even come up. "I hope so!" he replied.

Chariji has said that he himself disagreed many times with his Master, but that he did not ever disobey Him. This is an important distinction, and invites contemplation.

Chariji has also warned that a seeker should beware of any system headed by a supposedly changeless and "perfect" guru: "It indicates that everything beneath the guru is also frozen in place, like a stone pyramid." In Sahaj Marg, a Master is perfect in the way that the sky is always a perfect sky.

Why must a Master have a human form?

The Divine takes on human form because this is the form through which the rest of us all experience the universe. A Master faces the same problems we all face — earning a living, getting married, raising children, sickness, old age, death. God in His Heaven does not have to deal with these things, or with the treachery and deceit and pain and folly we find all around us in this world, and so God can give us no finer example than a Master in human form. By observing how a Master lives and works and plays, we can begin to see what is possible for us as human beings.

As Chariji once explained: "You see, so many of us are obviously so intensely interested in the spiritual life, but the difficulty is the very abstraction of the Goal and an even more potent difficulty is that we are unable to experience or to evaluate ourselves. Then I realized the importance of the Guru. Even though the Goal is an abstraction, indefinable, not locatable in space or time, yet we have before us a Guru, whom we believe sincerely and wholeheartedly to be an embodiment of all those virtues and qualities and he becomes a sort of sheet-anchor to direct us away from an abstract Goal to a concrete Goal, which is the Master, which is Divinity itself, so that this hiatus between That which we aspire for and the unknowability of That which we aspire for is removed in one stroke."

Secondly, a Master must have a human form to take on the samskaras of others and to remove their karma. This is one reason why saints and Masters often suffer ill health and other calamities beyond what may come to them naturally, for when they have finished with the bulk of their own karma, in their great love they are able to absorb and erase the karma of others.

Why can't we just rely on our inner voice? Also, couldn't we benefit from an ascended master, or from a great teacher in the past, like Christ or Buddha or Krishna or Mohammed? Why can't we learn from the great scriptures?

Or for that matter, I feel that everything and everyone should be taken as my guru; why not learn from life itself?

As for taking the inner voice or a departed soul to be our guru, Babuji has observed: "The practice of seeking inspiration or guidance from gods and demi-gods or from some departed soul and treating it as Guru or Master is in most cases very dangerous. Similar is the case with those who seek guidance from their inner voice as they call it. I have come across people who lay great stress upon their inner voice which they think to be the real guide in all controversial matters arising in the mind....Most of those who seek guidance from a departed soul are really following the dictates of their own unregulated and undisciplined mind. It is mere hallucination. If we develop this vicious habit we are lost forever. It leads us to constant mental worry and harassment....The inner voice is in fact the voice of the mind in its perfectly pure state. Unless the mind is cleared of all its pollutions and is brought to a state of perfect Peace and moderation, it can never reflect the inner voice. In fact, for one whose mind is pure, it is his inner voice alone that always speaks and the impulse from highly developed souls continues to flow to him continuously. The practice is thus evidently very dangerous and in most cases leads to disastrous results."

Babuji's words may seem strong, but they are backed up by teachers of many traditions. So our sense that we can be led by the "inner guru" is actually correct, as Babuji said, though such guidance can come only when we have stilled the mind to the degree that the Inner Voice even can be heard. Then we are able to proceed from sure inspiration or intuition, not from whims and impulses born from a still thriving ego. At best, we must admit that our so-called inner guru is an uncertain mix of Divinity and desire, Self and ego — and to verify the inner Voice, the assistance of an objective and experienced guide is invaluable. With such help, soon we gain experience and can tune out all the ego-static, discern the real Voice, and distinguish between illumined intuition and mere impulse.

Also, as Babuji suggested, the practice of taking ascended souls for our guru is often used to avoid the real difficulties of discipleship. The American scholar and Yoga practitioner Georg Feuerstein has made a similar observation: "The New Age craze of channeling is symptomatic of this approach, in which conveniently 'ascended' masters give all kinds of advice, which is usually quite innocuous and makes precious little demand for actual change. 'Dead gurus,' Da Love-Ananda once stated bluntly, 'can't kick ass.'"

Alas, this applies to the founders of the great religions as well: Buddha, Christ, Mohammed, Rama, Krishna and all the great Masters of the past are now, let us admit it, principally encountered in books. Even if we commune with them in meditation or prayer, we cannot observe them living in our own world of traffic jams and laundromats, not in the way that their direct disciples could witness them living in the worlds of centuries past. And noble as their teachings are, no book can take the place of the living presence of those masters as they lived with their disciples: "And the Word was made flesh and dwelt among us, and we beheld His glory," recorded John. The Sufis understand this, too: "Ten minutes in the company of the Friend," they say, "is better than ten thousand years in a library."

As for the notion that "everything, every situation, and everyone around us is the Guru": Again, this is true — but again, only *after* Realization. Before this, we may surely get guidance, and have many teachers, but we should not consider these as gurus (as Ram Dass observed, "Teachers point the way; the Guru is the way"). Vivekananda was typically fierce about this romantic dodge: "'Sermons in stones, books in brooks, and good in everything' is all very true as a poetical figure; but nothing can impart to a man a single grain of truth unless he has the undeveloped germ of it in himself. To whom do the stones and brooks preach sermons? To that human soul the lotus of whose holy inner shrine is already about to open. And the light which causes the beautiful opening of this lotus comes always from the good and wise teacher. When the heart has thus been opened, it becomes fit to receive teachings from the stones or the brooks."

Even in so-called "teacherless" traditions like that of Krishnamurti, which emphasize techniques over teachers, one could argue that ultimately those teachings are legitimized and embodied in the example of the teacher. The Buddha at his death told his disciple Ananda that not he, but his teachings would now "be the raft," yet the Buddha's teachings are drawn from his own experience and would have no value if he had not set an example and practically demonstrated the possibility of Realization for all of us.

So let us accept that a proper guide is essential if we wish to approach the highest reaches of human potential. And let us conclude with the words of Swami Vivekananda that are as pertinent today as they were when he spoke them to some American friends in 1895: "Be grateful to books and teachers without bondage to them, and worship your guru as God, but do not obey him blindly. Love him as much as you will, but think for yourself....Nothing can be done without a guru. In fact, great danger ensues....There is no reason why each of you cannot be a vehicle of the mighty current of spirituality. But first you must find a teacher, a true teacher, and you must remember that he is not just a man. You may get a teacher in the body, but the real teacher is not in the body. He is not the physical man; he is not as he appears to your eyes. It may be that the teacher will come to you as a human being, and you will receive the power from him. Sometimes he will come in a dream and transmit the spiritual ideal to you. The power of the teacher may come to us in many ways. But for us ordinary mortals a human teacher must come, and our preparation must go on till he comes."

TRANSMISSION

What is Transmission?

Transmission is the utilization of Divine energy for the transformation of man. In Sanskrit it is called *pranahuti* — from *prana* (life-force) and *ahuti* (to offer, to infuse). Chariji has spoken of it this way: "Transmission is *Pranasya Prana* — the 'Prana of Prana.' The Prana of the Divine is poured into your prana." This can be accomplished by an adept closely connected to the Source, one who has the ability to transmit from the center of his or her existence the "life of life" to the center of existence of another individual.

Long before Einstein's well-known equation $e=mc^2$ established a relation between energy (e) and matter (m), yogic science had studied the interplay of energy (*prana*) and matter (*prakriti*). Prana enlivens the universe and congeals as prakriti. Even though we cannot detect certain radio wavelengths or ultraviolet vibrations without proper instruments, still it is said that these energies are always flowing everywhere and at lightspeed (denoted as c in Einstein's equation). Just so, though only a few may consciously be tuned to send or receive prana, this flow of

Divine Grace is also unceasing and omnipresent. A Master can direct this flow in the most subtle manner for specific work not only on individual human beings, but also for the purposes of Nature across the multiverses — the inner universes and the universe or universes without.

Among the many things Babuji has said and written about the wonderful discovery of pranahuti is this: "Power of transmission is a yogic attainment of a very high order by which a yogi can infuse through his own will-force, the yogic energy or Godly effulgence within anyone and remove anything unwanted in him or detrimental to his spiritual progress. He can exercise this power not only on those assembled around him but on those, too, who are away from him. The power can be utilized in any way at any time. One who has got command over this power can, at a glance, create temporarily or permanently, a condition of the mind which is far ahead of the existing condition of the mind of an abhyasi and which otherwise will require a lifetime to be achieved. It is not a vain assertion, but a bare fact and may at any time be practically verified by anyone who pleases to do so. Sages have often through the power of transmission changed the entire nature of a man at a mere glance. The wonderful examples of the great sages like my Master, Samartha Guru Shri Ram Chandraji Maharaj of Fatehgarh, Swami Vivekananda, and others offer ample proof of it."

So others besides the Master or Sahaj Marg preceptors may transmit?

Of course. In a way, every one of us transmits. As Babuji said, if you sit next to a madman or a murderer, even an insensitive person will begin to experience uncomfortable feelings. If we sit next to a saint, we will feel peaceful and calm. The same holds true even for places and inanimate objects: we will feel the atmosphere of a slaughterhouse differently than the atmosphere of a cathedral. Granted, this is not pranahuti as it is understood in Sahaj Marg, but what Babuji described as the radiating vibration of *paramanus*, or subtle particles. If the atmosphere or aura of a place is like the light of a candle, then transmission may be compared to a beam of laser light. Though few may have consciously experienced direct transmission, many have felt the inexplicable "vibrations" in the proximity of certain people or places.

Nature's work is done only by permission. As indicated earlier, the highest saints and sages work harmoniously as a group, and are far away from the little sectarian squabblings of their followers. This is why obedience is an essential aspect of training, because work done at the highest level must be in accordance with Divine decree. It is one thing, for example, for a small college radio station to transmit to three or four blocks around the campus, and quite another for a 100,000-watt clear-channel superstation to transmit across several states. You might say that a kind of Celestial Regulatory Commission is in operation to keep the transmissions on the proper channels, and not conflict with other vibratory levels! Those beings who are permitted by Nature to transmit prana across the widest range and broadest scope must be absolutely trustworthy, given the enormous capacity at their command.

How is pranahuti different from other traditions of the transference of energy called **shabd** *or* **abhisheka** *or* **shaktipat** *or* **diksha,** *or even the giving of* **mantrams?**

Babuji has further described pranahuti as a "forceless force" or "powerless power" not because it brings no result, but because of its absolute subtlety, in that pranahuti is not tinged with materiality. In fact, Babuji knew that in spirituality what is most subtle is most effective. Pranahuti is devoid of all attributes, including even the *shakti* or power that informs *shaktipat*, or the vibrations of light and sound associated with the *shabda* of the Siddha Yoga tradition. Nor is the transmission from Master equivalent to what is called *diksha* or *abhisheka* in other traditions, since pranahuti does not confer or imply any kind of initiation by the Guru. Indeed, abhyasis frequently have experiences of power and divine light or splendor and the *ajapa* of hearing "soundless-sound" of the Universe as a reaction to pranahuti, but these experiences are just that — experiences. Wonderful as they may feel, they come and they go, like all experiences, and have little to do with real progress in spirituality. As such, these experiences are considered irrelevant and unnecessary in Sahaj Marg, and though we may have wondrous visions or develop other *siddhis* or paranormal powers in our practice, abhyasis are advised to let them all drop away, and to move on toward the Center unencumbered by even these samskaras!

The desire for powers or conditions like peace and bliss, or attempting to repeat some wonderful experience we once had in meditation only delays our progress. These tendencies or desires pull us away from what is happening right here and right now. Pranahuti is the flowing of Divine current. As such, it is unceasing, very gentle, and so fine and subtle that even the most sensitive recipient will not actually feel pranahuti itself, but only its effects as they gradually unfold in our lives.

Then is the method of transmission in Sahaj Marg a new one?

Yes and no. The technique of transmission is said to have existed for some ten thousand years, far before even Lord Rama's time in Bhaarat, presently known as India. It fell into disuse as generations passed, but is said to have been rediscovered by Lalaji Saheb as a perfect technique for our time. Babuji further refined the daily practices of Sahaj Marg, and passed the art of pranahuti on to Chariji.

Are the introductory sittings not considered initiation? Does initiation exist in Sahaj Marg? If so, why does Master initiate some abhyasis and not others?

The introductory sittings are just that: an introduction to the practice. By definition, you can become an abhyasi only by following the practice or abhyas yourself. Introduction does not mean initiation.

Initiation traditionally has implied that there is a lifelong or even eternal bond of responsibility established between the Guru and his disciple. Suppose initiation does occur these days in Sahaj Marg. Should we not leave it to the Master to decide when we are ready? Initiation is the prerogative of the Master, not the disciple. A four-year-old child may declare that she is ready to get married, and her father will smile and suggest that perhaps she should wait a while.

A second understanding of initiation might be the beginning of the movement of the soul, or *yatra*, in point one of the heart region, indicating a shift to a new level of consciousness. This initiation happens when sufficient interest is developed in the spiritual pursuit, and the spiritual heart of an abhyasi begins to soften and open to the Master's grace. Initiation in this sense happens when the time is right, whereas introduction is what happens when we start Sahaj Marg with three sittings.

Please describe the yatra, or journey. How do we know our position or approach, that is, at which point we are supposed to be?

Please see Babuji's *Towards Infinity* for a discussion of the yatra. As far as knowing our own "position," we cannot, just as we cannot see our own faces without some external help. For this, the Master can serve as our mirror.

Knowing position or approach is of no use for most abhyasis. Chariji has said himself that he never bothered about it when he was an abhyasi; for him it was enough that he was obeying his Master! It is fine for us to take an interest in the spiritual process and try to verify as much as we are able to for ourselves, but anxiety or pride or disappointment over their so-called approach has proved disastrous for many abhyasis. The Source has no points, no chakras. At that stage, there is no yatra, no moksha, no delusion, no enlightenment, no master, no abhyasi, no human, no divine, no samadhi, no maya, no Sahaj Marg, no Shri Ram Chandra Mission, no past, no present, no future.

Try to imagine that Stage.

Morning Meditation

What is so special about meditating at dawn? What if my work or family schedule does not permit this?

Chariji has said that during the time called *sandhya* when night meets day and day meets night, there is a balance in Nature. The morning sandhya is called *Brahmamuhurtham*, the hour of Brahman, and has traditionally been considered an auspicious time for communion with the Source. Experience and intuition can confirm this for anyone, no matter what their culture. When we meditate at that point of balance in nature, we are calm and clear, and nature itself helps us achieve the goal more quickly.

Modern life does not always allow this for everyone, and Sahaj Marg suggests that if it is not possible to meditate before dawn because of job or family demands, then simply to do so at the beginning of your day, whatever time that may be. But simply staying up late to watch television hardly qualifies as a reason to miss the irreplaceable opportunity of meditating in the gray of dawn. The first maxim, which asks abhyasis to rise before dawn, may seem daunting at first, but if there are no contradicting family duties or occupational demands, it is really very easy for an abhyasi to adjust his or her daily schedule to this natural rhythm. All we have to do is give it a try, and see for ourselves.

How is Sahaj Marg meditation different from just sitting silently and trying not to have thoughts?

In Sahaj Marg meditation we do not simply sit blankly with the mind in a dull or stunned condition, nor do we try to stop the mind from thinking, for merely being without thoughts is not the goal of Sahaj Marg practice. Though our meditation is indeed inner-directed, it is also devoid of all trying, or any forceful effort of concentration. Sahaj Marg meditation requires at the same time both strenuous effort and also no-effort on the part of the abhyasi, what we might call a kind of effortless-effort, attention without tension, or relaxed intensity. Thus, we favor absorption rather than concentration, which zeroes in on a single thought and tries to exclude all others.

Absorption simply allows thoughts to follow their own restless nature, arising and swarming and disappearing, without any attempt on our part to suppress them, and without our becoming either worried by unpleasant thoughts or fascinated with pleasing ones. If we simply remove our attention from the thoughts we will find that often they go away all by themselves. It is like diving beneath the turbulent surface of the sea to a depth where all is still and calm. Though the surface-mind may still be agitated and disturbed by the wind of thought, we are no longer caught in the turbulence of that surface, but are rather identified with the Deep. Although thoughtlessness might result from meditation in Sahaj Marg, that is not its goal. We are simply present to wait in stillness while Divinity becomes us.

To explain meditation to one unlettered man, Babuji asked him what he would do if the Master announced he was coming to visit his house as a guest. The man replied that he would clean up his house, and that poor as they were, he and his wife would prepare the best meal they could afford for the Master. And what would you do, Babuji asked, if the Master was late?

"Oh, Sir," said the man, "I would wait for my Master to arrive!"

"That," said Babuji, "is meditation."

Please explain what is meant by "the Divine light in the heart" we are supposed to meditate upon. How is this done? What are we supposed to see?

As explained in Sahaj Marg literature, we are not asked to do anything as crude as to visualize this Light — for example, to imagine a three-petaled flame or a glorious aura or anything like that. Babuji explained that it is not light, but the *idea* of Divine Light we envision at the place where our physical heart is beating. It is so subtle that he described it as "light without luminosity."

A basic truism of destiny is that we become that which we think in our heart, and this process is amplified by the intensity of meditation. The goal in Sahaj Marg is to become one with God, and yet it is impossible for the human mind to conceive of that which is without form, without color, without sound, power, substance, movement, space, or any other attribute of perception. This is called a "negative definition" for that which is really indefinable, which Babuji called the Base, the Source, the Illimitable, the Impersonal Absolute, because since we cannot say what it is because the Source is beyond the limits of language, we can indicate what it is by saying what it is not. This is the rationale of the formula of jnana yoga, the yoga of knowledge, which declares about the Supreme only these words: *Neti, Neti* — "Not this, not that!"

Therefore, since merging with the Source is the Goal of Sahaj Marg meditation, and since we cannot meditate directly on that which is beyond human thought (given the limited and limiting nature of human perception) our Master decided that the most subtle thought possible to use as the resting place or point of return for our mind during meditation was not just Divine light, but the *idea* of Divine light.

Practically speaking then, we begin meditation with the *sankalpa*, or willed-thought, of Divine light in the heart. We begin with this idea, then we simply sit and wait. We need not go on repeating the thought like some mantra; once is enough. It is like flicking the wall switch to turn on the light in a room: we need not keep hitting the switch once the lights are on. After that, there is nothing else for the mind to do. Simply rest, undistracted, in Divine light. Instead of internally staring at the heart area, just let there be light there, all by itself. Easy, relaxed, no effort. Don't try to make it happen. Just notice the light that is already there. Don't try to catch it or hold it, just let it be there by itself. If you get caught up in the surface tides of thought, that's okay, just recognize it and let yourself drift back into the original stillness.

Above all, as long as you are doing the practice as it is given, do not worry about what occurs during meditation. If you find you're having many thoughts, that's all right. Sometimes the mind, like the ocean, is calm; at other times, it is stormy. This is the nature of the mind, so just let it be. Try to observe what arises without attachment to what you may have wanted or expected. Meditation need not be seen as a test or a performance; instead it can be regarded as an agreeable adventure full of surprises — and sometimes meditation can even be fun. Why not? As our Masters have brilliantly seen and stated, "Everything that happens in meditation is good." No need to divide things into good and bad, or to assume that some states or emotions or thoughts are proper for meditation, while others are not. Such distinctions no longer pertain in the place where Sahaj Marg meditation happens.

You say we begin with an initial thought or **sankalpa,** *and then we sit with an attitude of inner attention. This sounds similar to Zen* **shikan taza** *("simply sitting")* **zazen** *meditation or Yogic* **vipassana** *(witnessing or insight) or even Tibetan* **dzogchen** *("great perfection") meditation. Is Sahaj Marg meditation like these — or, how is it not?*

All these are advanced forms and very good methods, and do share essential qualities of Sahaj Marg meditation such as effortless-effort, non-attached observation, gentleness, and creating a space between our Big Mind and the restless dreaming-scheming mind of our everyday ego. Like these methods, Sahaj Marg meditation allows one to begin to wake up from the *maya* or delusion that we are separate, alienated little egos struggling against the world "out there."

However, there are three small but significant differences: Sahaj Marg meditation is in the tradition of Raja

Yoga, which emphasizes mind and thought, yet our practice is centered in the heart and is sweetened by love. Indeed, Divine Love is one way to describe the indescribable energy called *prana*. Sahaj Marg meditation is not simply a witnessing of interior phenomena as they pass as in the mindfulness techniques, or a way of negation, the no-soul/no-goal endeavor of the certain Buddhist practices (though others do include *bodhicitta* and compassion).

Second, the transmission of prana from one Soul through another to another soul, is the second and quintessential distinction of Sahaj Marg meditation. It is this transmission, this pranahuti, that makes Sahaj Marg meditation unique.

A third feature of the Sahaj Marg system is the evening cleaning, which will be discussed in the next section. The cleaning is an essential aspect of the practice, without which real progress would be difficult or impossible.

Can I play music during meditation? Can I meditate with my eyes open? Can I try and think of good things? Can I lie down and meditate? Can I chant a mantra?

Sahaj Marg says that God is simple, and the Way to God is also simple. This is a great difficulty for many of us, who prefer to have strenuous or exotic or diverting rituals or practices — our busy minds want something to do! But in Sahaj Marg meditation, there is nothing for the ego to busy itself with, thinking that its activities can bring about some Result. So please just do the practice as you have been instructed. It is a light and efficient craft. There is no need to add anything to it, just as there is no need to put stone gargoyles on a canoe.

What about the place where I meditate. Is having a special room for* puja *(worship or meditation) necessary or helpful?

It is good to have a room, or corner, or some regular place in your home dedicated and set aside for meditation, if this is possible. Over time, the special atmosphere there will come to assist you as you continue to fill it with thoughts of the Divine day after day.

It is equally true that meditation in Sahaj Marg is an internal process, and we soon are able to remain unaffected by the environment outside us. Hence we need not attempt to change the outer environment during meditation. It is not the style of Sahaj Marg to require music or incense or special pillows or postures or any other special effects for meditation to take place. Nor do we always have to retreat to an ashram or to some sanctuary of holy silence. Sahaj Marg emphasizes ordinary life as sadhana and says that meditation is a natural activity and can take place anywhere. Even if the children are making a racket in the next room, or traffic is blaring outside, we meditate wherever we are. After some practice, the outer world does not distract. The day may come when we realize that the entire universe is our puja room.

Can I do the morning meditation for fewer than thirty minutes? Why is meditating the full hour preferred?

Babuji requested that meditation in the morning be done for one hour. However, one can begin with thirty or forty minutes and gradually increase it to one hour. When we begin meditating, the mind is made to go from an agitated to a quiet state, and this takes time. So in the first few minutes of meditation, we are usually just thinking and not

75

meditating. It takes some time for the mind to settle down to a quiet state. When we meditate for thirty minutes or less, we hardly meditate during that time. So we should try to sit for as close to an hour as possible, and give our thoughts sufficient time to calm and settle down. Then we are better positioned to see through the lake of our minds, so to speak, clear to the Soul or Ground of our Being.

Incidentally, we should not sit for more than one hour. As Chariji says, if a potato takes twenty minutes to cook, then we have to cook it precisely for that time. Otherwise, we are either under-cooked or over-cooked. It might be helpful to purchase an inexpensive timer, set it for one hour, and not get up till it goes off.

In the beginning, abhyasis usually want to be allowed to meditate for less than the recommended time — few ask to be allowed to meditate for *more* than one hour! But after some time, many abhyasis will find it is easy to meditate for one hour, and in fact, that the difficulty lies in returning from meditation.

The practice is so simple. There seems to be no training in Sahaj Marg.

Some people get this curious idea because in Sahaj Marg there are no meditation classes, no lectures, no mantras, no yogic postures, no special clothes, no changing of names, no training fees, and no special titles awarded in Sahaj Marg. The practice is simple, yes. Easy, no.

Nonetheless, sincere and regular participation does give a practical form of training to establish lasting growth. That is why Sahaj Marg is called a *system*: It offers a complete, systematic approach for spiritual training in the midst of everyday life. The Sahaj Marg system includes the daily meditations, keeping a diary, reading the literature, attending weekly satsangh, going to retreats at SRCM ashrams, receiving regular sittings with a preceptor, doing volunteer work if you wish, and above all, interacting with the spiritual guide by letter and whenever possible in person.

Eventually we may find that Sahaj Marg, instead of being defined by certain activities, becomes a natural way of living. Gradually, we come to see that the practice of Sahaj Marg is not one of many compartments in our lives, it *is* our life, which daily becomes more and more free of care and heaviness. We learn to deal with all that comes our way like the Master himself does, and we react less and less like slaves of circumstances or heredity. The daily practice of Sahaj Marg meditation becomes a foundation to build such a masterful life.

In Sahaj Marg, the Master, both internal and external, trains without training, just as he teaches without telling. This subtle process goes on all the time; it is happening quietly and unceasingly even when we don't recognize it — while we are at work or driving a car, even while we are asleep — all through the subtle Grace of our Master.

CLEANING

What is "cleaning" in Sahaj Marg? How is it different from meditation? Why isn't meditation alone enough?

In Sahaj Marg, "cleaning" refers to the technique whereby an abhyasi utilizes his or her will power for the purpose of removing subtle distortions, tendencies, impurities, coverings, or any other impediments to spiritual development. Cleaning is part of every abhyasi's daily practice, and is performed at the end of the day's work, usually at dusk, or before supper. Cleaning may also be assisted by preceptors or the Master himself in individual or group sittings.

Just as water is used for drinking and for bathing, so pranahuti may be used for nourishment (meditation) and for purification (cleaning). Chariji has repeatedly stressed the absolute necessity for cleaning for anyone who hopes to develop spiritually — indeed, he has often said the need for cleaning is more pressing even than the need for meditation, though both are necessary and are integral to the Sahaj Marg system. Without cleaning, we are doomed to endlessly repeat the same habits and patterns over and over, even across lifetimes.

Regarding the relation between cleaning and meditation, Chariji has given the simple analogy of a motor car. Even if the car's engine (which is the mind) is working properly, without petrol the car will go nowhere. Just so, we require not mere intellectual stimulation to move toward Reality, but we must actively practice meditation and open our hearts to receive the Grace of divine transmission. Yet even then, with its working engine and full tank of gas, the car will go nowhere if it is stuck in mud or if the road is obstructed. This can be compared to the habits or proclivities that despite our best efforts always seem to drag us back. Thus, cleaning is absolutely essential.

Like the morning meditation, the evening cleaning is accomplished by our initial sankalpa, or thought-plus-will, that Divine Grace is washing through our system, and the impressions of the day are leaving the back like smoke or vapor. Again, there is no need to force this thought or repeat it like a mantra — our initial intention is quite sufficient to carry the work through. Simply begin with the sankalpa as described above and then observe the process at work. Remember that thought is powerful and that we become that which we meditate upon, so please keep the focus on the wind of Divine light before you, not the grossness behind you. Do not make the mistake of trying to analyze or think about whatever impressions may be leaving you. The thoughts and memories that so often arise during cleaning may simply be brushed aside.

We exert our will, but this does not mean that we force the cleaning as if it were some sort of penance to be endured. It is nothing of the sort. To correct any feeling of work or effort on our part during the cleaning, we can remind ourselves at the outset that the work has already been accomplished for us, for at a certain level of Reality this is actually true. We can hold in our hands a book or a cassette of a movie that is already completed, beginning, middle, and end. At the same time, we must turn the pages of the book or watch the frames of the movie to bring them into our personal experience.

To be truthful, many abhyasis do not enjoy cleaning. Some even find it difficult or tedious. But practice will demonstrate that the benefits of regular cleaning are considerable. Habits that have plagued us all our lives drop away with ridiculous ease, fears and obsessions bid farewell, and we begin to experience a balance and freedom and health that even the most expensive and sophisticated therapies are unable to provide — and all this results from a daily practice using faith, imagination, and will, assisted by the Grace of the Master. This is the method called, in the simplicity of Sahaj Marg, *cleaning*.

What if I miss a day's practice? Can I combine cleaning and meditation the next day?

If we miss a day's practice, we can do the cleaning for a few minutes before the morning meditation the next day. But this should be only for special occasions, and should not become a habit. Every time we use our will in small ways, it gets stronger, and every time we avoid using it, it becomes weaker. As we develop Constant Remembrance, we become better able to remain in a naturally balanced and meditative mood throughout the day.

Abhyasis are not allowed to indulge in dramas of guilt and repentance. This is a waste of time and energy. Whether we have missed practice for one day or two weeks or ten years, each day is a new day. If you find you have lapsed in your practice, simply get back to work. Sahaj Marg deals with "right here, right now," and every day you practice you become a new abhyasi. We should not miss opportunities, but practice consistently with firm resolve to go all the way. As long as we are honest with ourselves and with Master, our slips will not become falls.

What does samskara mean?

The Sanskrit concept of *samskara* ("activator," or imprint) refers to the way that the impressions formed in us by our past thoughts and actions tend to govern and precipitate our future thoughts and actions. Over time these samskaras or impressions solidify into tendencies and become patterns and habits, which in turn create new habits and also filter our view of reality. Consider the familiar example of three people looking at a tree. An artist would probably admire its beauty and think of transferring the image to canvas; a businessman might see the same tree as potential lumber and think of it in terms of board-feet and money, an arsonist might think what a nice blaze he could get if he set the whole thing on fire. So how each of us views and reacts to the same situation depends on what our past has been. Our response to the present moment is shaped by our motives and desires, like the three people of our example. Past impressions are the reason we are what we are today, and the impressions that we form today will in turn determine what we become in the future.

Babuji explained the entire concept of samskara with typical brevity: "Samskara is a density of thought created by our action."

Please say more about how impressions are formed. What is the difference between a habit and a samskara?

Impressions are formed during the interplay of conscious actions and reactions in everyday life. For example, if we see a violent accident on the street, the heaviness of that action can remain for days. Sahaj Marg psychology does not view impressions *per se* as good or bad in a moral sense; they are simply traits we all acquire through the repetitive actions of desire. Even those samskaras which are considered beneficial or noble, such as a tendency to work hard or give help to the poor, are as confining as those that give rise to so-called "bad" habits. All habitual reactions, whether beneficial or harmful, cover, distort, or stain the original clarity and purity of the Big Mind. As Babuji observed, it does not matter whether the bars of our prison are made of iron or of gold, the prison is still a prison.

Until samskaras are cleared away, we cannot consider ourselves as free, for we remain as slaves to our own habits and desires. Just as water will create ruts and riverbeds for itself by its continued flow down the same channels, so the mind creates samskaras by past thoughts and ways of perceiving. When future thoughts come, they tend to be forced into the same ruts created by past mind-events; hence samskaras become activators of future actions — or reactions, to be more precise.

Though the cleaning practices in Sahaj Marg do not remove habits directly, because habits are the outward expressions of samskaras, they do clear away the inner conditions that give rise to these habitual patterns of action. Thus, while cleaning makes freedom from habits possible, the completion of the work, the part called character development, is left to the abhyasi. A Master will never do for a disciple what the disciple must do for himself. It is foolish to expect that if we merely sit before the Master and make no effort on our own that a permanent transformation will magically occur in our lives. The Master does his work; we must do ours. In short, without Divine transmission, change is impossible, but without the abhyasi's cooperation, Divine transmission will not be realized. Both are essential.

What does bhog *(bhoga or bhogam)* mean?

The Sanskrit word *bhog* is literally translated as enjoyment. In the specialized vocabulary of Sahaj Marg, bhog refers to the process of undergoing all the effects of samskaras, whether those results are enjoyment or misery. Bhog will occur whenever a suitable environment is found for a particular samskara to surface. When a samskara is formed, it can be likened to a tightly wound coil, waiting for its kinetic energy to be released by the process of bhogam whenever the environment provides the appropriate conditions. Samskaras are thus like seeds, awaiting the right circumstances to germinate and bear fruit.

Normally, samskaras can be released only by undergoing bhog in our lives, yet the problem is that we are endlessly creating new samskaras daily by our repetitive patterns of desire and activity. This unfinished business of bhog and samskara becomes an endless cycle, and may be one way to understand the theory of the driving force in reincarnation.

The only other way that samskara may be removed is through the grace of a Realized Master. In Sahaj Marg, this is accomplished though the process of cleaning.

Can we do the evening cleaning for less than thirty minutes?

The evening cleaning should be done for the full thirty minutes. Please do not cheat yourself.

Can we clean at any time during the day if we feel we need it? Can we do these extra cleanings for less than thirty minutes?

Experience shows that when the practice is adhered to with sincerity and regularity, the need for extra cleanings is rarely felt. But if something happens or if we simply feel the need to do more cleanings, then it is all right to clean for five or ten minutes. We must understand that when the cleaning is done in the evening, use of will is necessary. We sit with the sankalpa (willed-thought) that the samskaras we may have acquired since our last cleaning are being washed away in the flow of divine energy coming from the front, and are disappearing from our back like smoke or vapors. This strengthens our will and when we go about our business in constant divine thought, the need for extra cleanings should drop off.

How can we know if our condition is "gross," or if we need cleaning?

It's a good idea not to become too concerned about our own condition. First, focusing on our own gross condition tends to solidify what may be only fantasy into reality. As mentioned above, remember that a law of the inner universe is that we always become that which we think in our hearts, and so the same process that lifts us to the divine in meditation can also mire us in misery if we "meditate" on our failings. This is the wisdom behind Babuji's famous statement about sin, that "the only real sin is to brood upon sin." A second caution against trying to dissect our current condition is that finally, we cannot know our own condition. For this, we require the true mirror of a Master.

That said, most abhyasis can easily develop an intuitive feel for when they are open and happy and light and when they are not. Love expands, it feels soft and light. Anger or lust or greed cause the spirit to contract and harden. A simple test, then, is to look within and intuitively gauge whether we feel contracted, dense, hardened, heavy, closed — or expanded, light, soft, and open. We may feel somewhere in between, but our true condition is the one we experience when we are at our best. These conditions can change quite a bit as we move through various spiritual regions, so we should simply take note of the fluctuations and move on toward our Goal, which is beyond any condition.

I am not clear on the difference between memory and impression. Will I forget things with cleaning?

We lose only that which prevents us from returning to our Original Condition, which is Divine. We will retain whatever is necessary for us to function in human life, including memory, but there will be no heaviness or attachment to the memories, and certainly no compelling quality, which is the characteristic of samskaras. Speaking from the level of Eternity, the only real memory we possess is that primordial memory of our Home.

Why should I imagine myself filled with light at the end of cleaning?

First, because as Spinoza put it, Nature abhors a vacuum. Therefore, at the end of the cleaning we imagine that a Divine Light or current of Grace is filling the vacuum created by impressions that have been washed away.

Second, we finish cleaning with a positive rather than a negative feeling, with the thought that the cleaning has been accomplished, and with our heart tuned to the Divine. We feel lighter when we complete our daily cleaning, and we finish each day feeling clear, calm, and balanced.

PRAYER

Why pray? I thought Babuji said, "Prayer is begging, meditation is having"?

On the subject of prayer in general, and how prayer comes into the practice of Sahaj Marg, Chariji has written: "To me it is a cry from inside, addressed to we know not whom, for the fulfillment of a need within. Take a tiny baby. It cries when it is hungry and its mother rushes to feed it. But does the baby know that it is hungry and that it should express its hunger? Surely not! It is a cry of nature from within for the fulfillment of a need which it does not know, and nature in the form of its mother responds from outside to fulfill the need expressed inarticulately by the baby. I would therefore define prayer as a call from nature within to Nature outside for the fulfillment of a need of which the self is not consciously aware. But the inner nature recognizes it and gives utterance to it.

"When Babuji said that prayer was begging, all he meant was that throughout the history of mankind, prayer has rarely risen above the attitude of begging to anything higher."

Five other hints regarding prayer:

1. Chariji has pointed out that praying for others is helpful in that it takes us outside of our own self-concern. This is what occurs, for example, during the Nine O'Clock Prayer that we are asked to take on voluntarily as part of our sadhana or practice. The Nine O'Clock Prayer is one aspect of our sadhana that we do not for ourselves especially, but for others. The use of prayer in Sahaj Marg helps guard us from becoming solipsistic or self-involved, and keeps us connected with others and the world around us.

2. Chariji has also explained that we need not presume to pray for God or Master to do this thing or that particular thing for someone, all we do is place the person we may be praying for in the presence of Master. The difference between ordinary petitionary prayer or vertical begging and the higher form of prayer that Sahaj Marg employs is succinctly explained by Chariji: "Most people say, 'Lord, please put Thy will behind my wish!' Whereas the real prayer says, 'Lord, Thy wish is my will.'"

3. Always remember that gratitude can open the heart that resentment has closed. Maxims Five and Seven remind us that the surest remedy for all the ills that beset us when we lapse into bitterness, hurt feelings, or anger is to remember the reality of our position in this world. When we see Reality clearly, gratitude is the natural response to our current situation, whatever it may be.

4. The secret of prayer is to pray as if the prayer has already been granted.

5. Remember that we do not pray to a God who is far away on some throne of a remote Heaven. The self in us which makes our prayer is also that Self which hears that prayer! Understood in this light, prayer is a Divine communication within: to pray is to commune with the One who abides in our own heart.

The first line of the Mission Prayer bothers me because I do not like praying to a human being, but only to God.

We should keep in mind that we have not been asked to agree with the Mission Prayer or to perform an exegesis or critical interpretation upon it as we go to bed at night; we are advised only to mentally repeat it a few times and then to meditate upon its meaning. Gradually, we may come to find that the Prayer is much more than a few simple words, and then we begin to absorb the essence of the prayer.

Babuji and Chariji have clarified on many occasions that God is the real Master, and it is to God that all prayers are addressed. You may also address your prayer to the Master within, if this suits you.

The second line of the Mission prayer bothers me because it sounds like a negative affirmation.

All that we do here is to state that we are creating the problems ourselves and that we recognize and accept that fact. Also, do not forget the promise of that little word *yet* in "We are yet but slaves of wishes..."! Naturally, we will still continue to have wishes, such as the wish that all our brothers and sisters be filled with love and devotion, but the important distinction here is that we will no longer be *slaves* of wishes.

The third line of the prayer: Why does it say "the only God and power"? Why is the Master equated to this?

"God" and "power" are seen as two, not one. The Origin is without any attributes, including power. This line really expresses a state of surrender. We are simply saying that we accept His guidance and express a readiness to hold His hand and let Him take us to our destination. The scriptures agree that only our chosen Guru holds the key to unlock God in a disciple's heart.

Taken together, the three lines of the Mission Prayer are simple statements of three facts:

A) The Goal of our life and our practice.

B) Our current approach to that Goal, along with the reason we are stuck where we now are.

C) The means to reach the Goal — how to make B become A.

Please explain the distinction between the cleaning meditation to remove samskaras and the use of the Tenth Maxim.

The evening cleaning is silent and works at both sub- and super-conscious levels of samskaric accretion. As such, cleaning is neither moral nor a-moral, since it does not deal directly with the our conscious existence of ethical concerns or morality. "Good and bad" do not pertain to the levels worked upon in the evening cleaning. As noted in the previous section, acts of kindness can be just as samskaric as acts of lust or anger — all must be cleaned. Thus, cleaning is Master's work, and is done for us.

The Tenth Maxim explicitly focuses on ethics, purity, and morality on the conscious level of human living. We are asked to honestly assess our day as we have lived it, and repent for wrongs committed knowingly or unknowingly. In Sahaj Marg, repentance simply means that we resolve not to repeat the same mistakes. This is work of character formation, and this the Master does not do for the disciple. This is the abhyasi's work.

Please note that the Tenth Maxim does not ask us to feel guilty; instead it asks us to "feel the presence of God," and feeling the presence of God is not bad! When we are asked to reveal ourselves before God, we do so with the ease and comfort of seeking help from our own mother or father, or in explaining our condition to our doctor. We simply state the facts of our day; no drama, no passion plays of guilt and penance are necessary. The idea of confession plays no role in the Tenth Maxim.

When we are learning to dance, we learn by realizing where we were unskillful in our attempts to learn this dance. We simply take note of our mistakes, practice the steps, and try to do better tomorrow. This is all that is meant by "beg forgiveness, repent and resolve." Thus, the Tenth Maxim becomes a simple and effective method that we can use to review and improve our behavior and bring it into harmony with our inner condition.

CONSTANT REMEMBRANCE

Why "Constant Remembrance"? I prefer "Constant Presence" or "Constant Mindfulness." "Remembrance" seems like a reference to the past. I feel we should be in the present only.

We shouldn't get too tangled in words, but try to appreciate truth. Even if we think we are remembering the past (or for that matter, predicting or envisioning the future) we always remain in the present moment. This is the Eternal Now of Constant Remembrance. Constant Remembrance occurs in the heart, and in that place we are beyond the tenses and demarcations of time. In this place, the past, present, and future are regarded from the view of the eternity.

As indicated in the discussion of cleaning, living in the ordinary mind is like watching a theatrical movie frame-by-frame and becoming caught up in the *maya* or illusion of connected motion. We cry or laugh over the *lila* or play of Light and Sound as the movie winds along from beginning to end. Drama requires three things: first, time to play itself out (a past, present, and future); second, desire (which in comedy will be fulfilled; in tragedy, frustrated), and third, a kind of hypnosis that allows us to willingly believe in actors parading before us on the screen or stage as real characters. Constant Remembrance, or Big Mind, is like holding the entire script or reel in view; seeing beginning, middle, and end simultaneously; and realizing that the whole charade is, after all, only the amusement of the Little Mind. Of course, Constant Remembrance allows us to return to our Little Mind whenever we like and enjoy the movie of our daily dramas — but we can also get up whenever we please and walk out of the theater. We are no longer chained to the seats of our relentless dramas, like the denizens of Plato's famous Cave.

Remembrance of Master means we remember who we really are. Constant Remembrance is nothing less than the practice of being a real or true abhyasi at all times in everything we do.

We are told to think that Master is doing whatever we happen to be doing, not ourselves. But how can I imagine Master doing bad things or having bad thoughts?

Try it and see what happens to the bad thoughts. Actually, for the abhyasi, there are no bad thoughts in the conventional sense — or good ones either, for that matter. Some thoughts and actions delay our progress and harm us; others help us along the way. That is all.

Once an abhyasi was absent from satsangh for a good while, and Lalaji asked why he was no longer coming around. The others told the Master that this particular fellow had returned to drinking, and was ashamed to appear before Lalaji. Lalaji said, "For this he is staying away? It is nothing! Bring him to me." The poor fellow was brought before Lalaji and began prostrating and begging forgiveness until the

Master told him to stop all that nonsense. Lalaji told him that if he wished to go into a bar and have a drink, it was fine: just think that Lalaji himself was taking the drink. Well, the fellow was delighted. What a Master! What a great practice! He went straight to the bar and ordered whiskey. Thinking of Lalaji, he raised the glass to his lips and drank — and the whiskey came right back out!

So whether you are, say, drinking a beer or cheating in business or committing adultery, or committing any action you know in your heart to be wrong and harmful, but feel that you cannot resist, simply imagine that the Master is doing these things in your place, and see what happens.

By the way, we should give the Master not only our "bad" thoughts and deeds but also our so-called "good" ones as well. Thus there is no place in the heart of an abhyasi for either shame or pride.

PRECEPTORS

Why does the Master need preceptors to help him?

The Master doesn't need preceptors to help; he allows preceptors to work. Among the many reasons for this permission for preceptors to participate in spiritual work are 1) so that not only abhyasis, but also the preceptors may themselves benefit, 2) so that abhyasis might begin to understand that divinity is within everyone (including preceptors), and 3) so that everyone might receive a greater degree of personal attention and particularized transmission and cleaning.

As Babuji once expressed it: "Preceptors are the arteries of the Mission connected to the heart."

What if no preceptor lives in my area? Can I still practice Sahaj Marg?

Certainly. Chariji is currently giving worldwide individual sittings each Friday at nine P.M. local time to every abhyasi who does not have a preceptor in his or her area. One can also consider setting up a time with a full preceptor for a long-distance sitting.

As for group meditations, abhyasis can get together and meditate even if no preceptor is present. Again, a full preceptor can be notified about group sittings, or abhyasis can hold satsangh knowing that in reality, the Master gives all sittings, whether a preceptor is present or not.

What if we do not like a particular preceptor? Should we report to Master if we feel preceptors are not doing their job?

If we feel that a particular preceptor's action or attitude is coming in the way of our spiritual progress, we can write to Master about it. If we feel that in some way a preceptor is seriously failing in his or her duty to the Master and to abhyasis, we owe it to the preceptor to refer the matter to Master for his help.

As abhyasis, we are practicing to become like the Master, and the Master is unmoved by personal likes and dislikes. The Master does not judge whom He accepts as abhyasis. We should try to reflect that attitude. We have not been appointed as spies, and we must always regard our own heart before deciding the best course to take in such a case. Our personal dislike for a particular preceptor can arise from many causes, in ourselves as well as in the preceptor. Spiritually speaking, whenever we have a strong reaction to anyone, it is a good idea to examine our experience, since the traits in others that trigger our particular samskaras may be an indication of their true nature, which we do not wish to accept in ourselves. This is not always true, of course, but basic psychological processes of transference, displacement, projection, and mirroring must at least be considered. By dispassionately observing our daily reactions to other people just as we observe thoughts that arise during meditation, difficulties not only with preceptors but with anyone can become a valuable teaching for the serious abhyasi.

It should also be noted that a preference and liking for a particular preceptor can be just as problematic for an abhyasi as a dislike. Both likes and dislikes must be transcended, and any undue aversion or attraction to a particular preceptor can disrupt the primary and original relation of all abhyasis, namely, the one they have with the Master. There can be no intermediary between an abhyasi and the Master; it is a direct one-to-one relationship for all of us. Though we may learn about the practice and get help from preceptors, our love and loyalty is reserved for the Master alone. It is a good thing when gratitude begins to dawn in an abhyasi's heart, and though we do well to feel grateful appreciation and respect for a dedicated preceptor, our heart belongs always and only to our Master. This is why Babuji gave this hint to abhyasis: "Give your mind to the preceptor and your heart to the Master."

It is a good thing to keep our interaction with the preceptors focused on spiritual matters as far as possible and to realize we need not socialize with them. One antidote to both disliking or to liking an individual preceptor is to put the Master in the place of any preceptor giving the sitting. (If you have not established a heartfelt connection with the Master, you may prefer to think that the transmission is coming to you from the Source itself.) Master connects us to the Source, and He provides transmission from the highest level. Putting Master in place of the preceptor is helpful not only for the abhyasi but also for the preceptor, since this is precisely the thought that preceptors make — that it is not they, but the Master in their place who gives each sitting — and if both the abhyasi and the preceptor are together in this, then the work of cleaning and transmission is much easier. It is an accurate thought, by the way, for in reality the Master is the one who gives each and every sitting in Sahaj Marg, whether we are at satsangh, or having an individual sitting with a preceptor, or meditating by ourselves.

Is there a difference in transmission from one preceptor to the next? Are some preceptors better than others? Are some preceptors more spiritually advanced than others?

As already noted, the transmission always comes from the Master. Since preceptors act merely as arteries, the essence of what is transmitted is no different regardless of who the preceptor is.

Preceptors need not be more spiritually advanced than the abhyasis who receive sittings from them. Master has designed the system so that a preceptor can assist an abhyasi who may be more spiritually advanced than the preceptor. Preceptors are like other abhyasis in that they have different personalities, skills, strengths and weaknesses — and, yes, different levels of knowledge, wisdom, emotional maturity, and spiritual advancement. As a general rule, preceptors do the best they can to assist their brothers and sisters with what they have available to work with, and with the transmission given through them by the Master.

Can abhyasis pick up negative stuff from a preceptor during a sitting? What if the preceptor's condition is not good? I feel vulnerable not knowing.

The abhyasi will receive nothing harmful from any preceptor, no matter what their condition may be, since it is the Master who directs the transmission. Preceptors are advised to do their practice diligently as abhyasis, including self-cleaning and receiving sittings from other preceptors. In this way they can continue to be clear and clean. But even if a preceptor fails to perform his work, the Master will take up the work and look after the abhyasi.

How should we meditate when receiving an individual sitting from a preceptor? Is it different for group sittings?

Begin with the thought of Light in the heart, just as you do in your morning meditation, and put the Master in place of the preceptor — or if you prefer, think that the transmission is coming to you directly from the Source itself.

What exactly is a "full preceptor"?

A preceptor is one who is permitted by the Master to train spiritual aspirants through pranahuti or yogic transmission under the Sahaj Marg system of Raja Yoga. Most preceptors are given "provisional" permission, which means that their permission can be withdrawn by the Master if he feels that they are not doing their job, whereas full preceptors are given "full" permission. Regarding the work, full preceptors might be likened to a fire hose, and provisional preceptors to a garden hose. The water traveling through both comes from the same Source, and is identical.

Like the hoses in our analogy, both full and provisional preceptors can transmit nothing without connection to the Source, and no preceptor owns whatever transmission flows through him or her. So one difference between full and provisional preceptors, then, is simply the volume that is able to flow through them. Both hoses can fill a tub, though one will do so a bit more quickly. The techniques any preceptor may use are determined by the Master.

What are the requirements to be a preceptor? How can I become a preceptor?

Sometimes when the Master feels that a preceptor is needed in a certain area he might select an abhyasi who is devoted, doing his or her own practice well, and willing to volunteer his or her time for the work.

Babuji said that abhyasis should not harbor the desire to become a preceptor, as this desire can retard progress since it diverts us from our real Goal. In fact, Master has indicated that the desire to become a preceptor is sometimes a sign of spiritual greed or even ego, both of which are detrimental in an abhyasi, and could be even more of a problem for him or her if the abhyasi becomes a preceptor. Please remember that preceptor work is *permitted* by the Master, it can never be *earned*. Master has humorously remarked that he sometimes appoints abhyasis as preceptors so that they might grow, or become more disciplined, or less self-centered.

So certain abhyasis are made preceptors as the next stage in their own spiritual training. As Master says, "The work teaches." This is why Chariji has told preceptors that they should thank the abhyasis who come to them for sittings, because they are helping the preceptors evolve and learn.

What does Master do to make an abhyasi into a preceptor?

The preparation of a person to be a preceptor usually consists of a number of intensive sittings from other preceptors (usually full preceptors) and a final sitting from the Master. What is opened in that sitting is Master's business, but he has hinted that transmission does not deplete the preceptor's own store of spiritual energy.

Can preceptors read our minds?

No. Please remember that preceptors are not fortune-tellers or psychics. The so-called "reading ability" of preceptors indeed grows keener with experience, but preceptors normally see nothing of what we have done or left undone. They may detect, however, the effects of behavior in the form of darkness, hardness, or grossness seen or felt in certain areas of the abhyasi's subtle body. This comes only so that the preceptor may better assist the abhyasi by removing samskaras. Experienced preceptors may sometimes even see and clean accumulations that occurred in past existences.

Preceptors don't seem special at all. They seem to be like ordinary people.

That is exactly what preceptors are — nobody special! If for no other reason than the fact that Master has trusted them with spiritual work, preceptors should be respected and heeded, but please excuse them if they sometimes fail to be wise and kind and knowledgeable. As already indicated, preceptors are also abhyasis going through the cooking process of sadhana like the rest of us, and are heir to all the flaws and follies that all human beings are prey to. Though they do their best to serve their Master, no preceptor can pretend to be an infallible supernatural hero. In giving sittings, the primary function of the preceptor is basically to do the unglamorous work of cleaning and cleaning and cleaning.

What kinds of things may we tell preceptors? What about confidentiality?

Preceptors are forbidden by Master to discuss anything that abhyasis have discussed at individual sittings or mentioned in confidence. This is an essential condition for trust. If a preceptor is heard speaking loosely of the confidences of another abhyasi or preceptor, he or she should be corrected at once, and the matter may be brought to the Master's attention.

As abhyasis, we can tell a preceptor anything we might tell a friend, but as a general rule, we should speak with preceptors primarily about matters regarding our spiritual practice. Preceptors are expected to know enough about Sahaj Marg to keep the Master from having to answer the same questions a thousand times. Personal matters can be discussed with the preceptor, if we feel comfortable about this, or with the Master directly through letters.

Please keep in mind, though, that preceptors are instructed by Master to refrain from giving advice. Preceptors are not therapists or counselors, and are forbidden to give medical, psychological, financial, or any other advice as part of the work permitted them by the Master, which is limited to the spiritual practice of Sahaj Marg only. Preceptors are happy to share their experience and strength with brothers and sisters, and even though they may not be masters, they can at least be humble examples of how an evolving abhyasi might live. In sum, the job of the Sahaj Marg preceptor is to help facilitate the direct interaction between the Master and the abhyasi.

SATSANGH

What does "satsangh" mean?

The word *satsangh* means "to be with the truth." In Sahaj Marg it refers to the group meetings. A satsangh usually consists of a session of group meditation, sometimes followed by readings from the various Masters, talks, or informal discussions. Satsanghs are usually held in a preceptor's home.

How often should I attend satsangh? Is it a requirement?

We should attend a satsangh at least once a week. If no preceptor lives nearby, abhyasis may still gather for weekly satsangh. Satsanghs are part of the practice of Sahaj Marg and should not be neglected.

I do not like groups. Can't I practice on my own and just get individual sittings? Is it really necessary for me to attend group meditations?

Sahaj Marg encourages abhyasis to treat fellow human beings as brethren and learn to share and grow together. Our inhibitions can become hurdles to our progress and the sooner we learn to work through them, the better. Sahaj Marg is not a path for recluses or misanthropes; abhyasis must learn to meditate both in solitude and among others. Indeed, some spiritual work can best be accomplished in our exchanges and even our conflicts with others. Learning to tolerate, respect, and ultimately to love others is no theoretical or academic exercise in Sahaj Marg — it is a practical reality, and along with normal family and working life, satsangh is the best training for this.

If one wishes to wash potatoes, sometimes it is faster to put them all in one big sack, rather than wash them one at a time in the river. Put the sack into the river, and as the potatoes rub and grind together in the current, simply allow them to wash each other. In this case, the sack is satsangh, the river is Master's transmission, and we can guess who the poor potatoes are!

Are there any rules or programs for satsanghs? For example, should there be readings from books or talks by abhyasis? I find that satsanghs vary from place to place and do not seem to have any set pattern.

Master has said, "We come together to meditate." Abhyasis are advised to arrive about thirty minutes before group meditation, if possible, and do their own individual cleaning. Preceptors who give satsangh are also requested to clean for thirty minutes prior to the group meditation, and the recommended time for group meditation is one hour. Meditation is the only essential for satsangh. Beyond this, there are no hard and fast rules for satsanghs. As Master once joked, "The only thing we should be rigid about is flexibility!" So there may be announcements, or readings, or talks, or informal discussions after meditation. Or as is sometimes the case, nothing at all is said, and once abhyasis have taken a few minutes to study their condition after the conclusion of meditation, everyone may simply rise and leave as they came — in silence.

As already suggested, the purpose of satsangh is to assist in each abhyasi's spiritual growth. We come together in the way that athletes come to a gymnasium — not to belong to some group, but to train individually together. Thus, it is a good idea for abhyasis to keep the purpose of satsangh in mind, and not to indulge in irrelevant talking before and after meditation. Even so, satsanghs can be relaxed and friendly events, sometimes silent, sometimes filled with laughter, always serious but never somber, where we are guided by love, sensitivity, and intuition.

Why must we wait for several hours before and after satsangh to have individual sittings?

Frankly, because individual sittings are not necessary after a group meditation. We need time to absorb the transmission of the satsangh. Master has also requested abhyasis not to get individual sittings for a few hours before satsangh, for this same reason. The half-hour just before satsangh, as already noted, should be spent cleaning.

What is the technique we should use in group meditations? Is it the same as when receiving individual sittings?

The technique is the same in receiving an individual sitting with a preceptor and in group sittings. Think that the Master himself is giving you a sitting. Begin with the idea of Light in the heart, as you do in your morning meditation. Open to that Light.

Why do men and women sit separately in satsangh?

It should be noted that men and women work together freely and naturally at all Sahaj Marg gatherings, but satsangh is a very special event, where precision and clarity are premium. From the preceptor's view, it has to do with unique male and female energies and vibration, and so helps proper transmission. Also, few are able to totally isolate themselves from the environment around them and slip into the depths of meditation easily. So in satsanghs, men and women sit separately to help them focus without distraction on the real Goal.

KEEPING A DIARY

I do not like writing. Is keeping a diary essential? What are the reasons to keep a spiritual diary?

Keeping a diary is very beneficial in our spiritual practice, which is why Master asks all abhyasis to do it. Writing a diary does three things for us: 1) it makes us sensitive to the meditative process and to our condition; 2) it allows us to detach from our busy ego-mind and establish a calm and objective witness-consciousness; 3) it becomes a testament of our own experience. This last is especially important during our first three months of testing the practice, because Sahaj Marg emphasizes practical experiment and direct experience. Thus, our diary becomes our own personally-verified scripture of the results of Sahaj Marg sadhana.

What sorts of things are we supposed to write in our diary?

We start by writing everything we see about ourselves, and soon the diary becomes a day-by-day record of our inner life, and how it affects or is affected by outer circumstances.

Experience will teach us. We should learn to remove all the opinions of ourselves and be ready to "bare the naked condition of our soul," as Babuji puts it. Doing this is a significant step in learning to accept ourselves as we are. Honest and objective diary-keeping can help to open our heart and remove our inhibitions.

Lalaji Maharaj has suggested ten areas to keep in mind when recording our diary:

1. Fresh ideas generated

2. Different kinds of feelings arisen

3. Special happenings or events

4. Peculiar signs observed in our profession

5. Dreams seen

6. Words heard inside

7. Changes or improvements in character

8. Coming across with the souls of saints in waking or sleeping state and the perception of their directions

9. Astral voices heard

10. Losing of worldly bondage and delusion (Maya)

WRITING AND VISITING MASTER

Can one meet the Master personally? How accessible is he?

Chariji resides in Madras, India, for four to five months each year. He travels all around the world and visits various centers and ashrams during the rest of the year. Abhyasis are encouraged to visit him as often as we can, either in Madras or during his travels. If we wish to accompany him during his travels or visit him in India, prior permission needs to be obtained and we may contact the preceptors regarding this. Master spends a lot of time at the Babuji Memorial Ashram when he is in Madras, and this is where most overseas abhyasis are quartered when they visit him in India.

Abhyasis who are able to visit "the lion in his own den" are exceptionally fortunate, for there are some things which can be learned from a Master in no other way than by close association, for the Guru teaches without telling. *Gurukulam* (or living as a family member with one's Master) is an ancient and essential boon of discipleship, and our Master graciously receives all who are blessed to join him in his day-to-day life.

Why should we write Master? After all, he is a Master. Shouldn't he already know whatever we might tell him?

Writing to Master regularly opens up our heart and removes any inhibitions we may have in approaching him. It also establishes a personal connection with the one who is the embodiment of our goal. So it is to our benefit to write to him. Master has said that our letters have nothing to do with "confession" or "revealing secrets." We simply put the facts of our spiritual condition before the Master just as we would describe physical symptoms to a doctor.

Further, though Master may perceive things in us, still he must know how we perceive these things ourselves, and how we report our own condition in response to his transmission.

Please remember: The work of Master and abhyasi is a cooperative partnership, and though he always performs his part, if we fail to do our part, the work cannot be completed, and what could become a masterpiece remains unavailable to the world.

How often should we write to Master? Doesn't he have enough to read already, with thousands writing him?

When asked this, Chariji said with a smile, "You do your job and let me do my job." It is true that Master receives thousands of letters, and the number keeps growing. So we should try to write concisely, to keep our letters as brief and clear as possible.

Does Chariji actually read all the mail himself? If we mark our letters "Personal & Confidential" will anyone besides Master read it?

Formal letters regarding administration of the Mission are opened by his secretary. Master does read the letters of all who write to him seeking spiritual guidance. The matters contained in letters marked "personal and confidential" remain thus. We should understand, however, that though they are read by Chariji, his secretaries or sometimes a translator may also need to see them for the purpose of a reply. Abhyasis are asked to recognize this necessity and to appreciate the enormous demands of the volume of correspondence Master undertakes daily.

What happens to my letters after Master has read them?

These letters go into the Mission's archives. It is a good idea to keep a copy of the letter for ourselves.

What is the format of the letter? Must it be typed? How long can it be?

It is recommended that letters be typed, or if this is not possible, printed clearly. Please try to stick to relevant facts, and if you can compress what you wish to say into "seed-form" as Master calls it, it will be helpful. Usually one page or less will do for most matters. Please put the date, your name, and your return address in the upper right-hand corner of every letter.

What sorts of things may we write Master about? Why can't we just ask a preceptor? I have a hard time when I attempt to write Master!

Then why not ask yourself why you have a hard time when you write to Master? The writing itself can be as revealing for us as any written response from Master might be. For this reason, some abhyasis write many letters to Master but only mail a few! Chariji said that when he felt reluctant to write to Babuji, it was usually because he had something he wished to hide. Sometimes writing a letter to Master can help us face and finish off concerns that have been nagging at us forever.

Preceptors are expected to be able to address basic questions dealing with our practice. It is perfectly acceptable to ask a preceptor, or any brother or sister, anything we wish to ask. Preceptors should sense when an abhyasi should write directly to Master concerning a spiritual experience or perhaps a question the preceptor is uncertain about, and will advise the abhyasi accordingly.

Basically, we may write to our Master everything related to our spiritual practice, or anything in our personal lives that we think is important to our spiritual growth. Here, as elsewhere in Sahaj Marg, there is no hard and fast rule. Let your heart guide you.

Can we simply photocopy our diary and mail it to him?

It is all right to mail a photocopy portions of one's diary, preferably enclosed with a typed summary.

I've written Master and asked him questions, but I did not receive a reply. Why? Should I write again?

It is not necessary to write him again. Letters that need written replies will receive them. Furthermore, Chariji has said that whether an abhyasi gets a written reply or not, all letters to the Master receive a response. Experience can prove this statement true.

Master says that when we ask a question and get an answer from someone else, we have merely gotten an answer, not a solution. Perhaps the best way is to place a problem that is vital to our spiritual growth before Master, and wait for the solution in our lives. Again, experience will soon prove to us that the most convincing answers are the truths we realize in our heart, not the words we read on a page.

What if we feel the need to contact Master about some urgent matter? What is the best way to do this? Can anyone call Master?

Urgent matters may be sent by Fax through Master's secretary. Her number in Madras is published in various Sahaj Marg magazines, including the quarterly *Constant Remembrance*, or you can get it from a preceptor. If the need is both dire and urgent — we might even say a matter of life-and-death — then we can telephone Chariji. As a matter of tact and etiquette, abhyasis might consider contacting the local preceptor before phoning Master, and seek their confirmation regarding this recourse. The fact is, that everyone — from the day-old beginner in Sahaj Marg to the most advanced associate — has the same direct relationship with the Master, for beyond all the roles and outer forms Master looks to the heart, where all souls are one.

THE MISSION

Why is there a need for an organization to impart spiritual training?

From a purely spiritual level, there is absolutely no need for any physical organization. But since human beings have bodies which must be moved around and fed and sheltered, then a physical organization, with ashrams and offices and dormitories and all the rest, comes into being.

Sahaj Marg serves the whole human being, physical as well as spiritual. Substance, however, is always more important than structure. Regarding organization of the Mission and physical sites for meditation, we are guided by the simplicity of Babuji, who emphasized "minimum physical comfort and maximum spiritual benefit."

Keep in mind that every living creature is also a physical organization or organism. The body that is Shri Ram Chandra Mission reflects the organic principle in nature. Thus, the Mission's management is designed by the Master to remain in tune with the natural order — that is, simple and functional.

What is the legal structure of the Mission?

Shri Ram Chandra Mission is a registered non-profit corporation in many countries, including the United States. The by-laws in each country are derived from that of Shri Ram Chandra Mission in India. The purpose of SRCM as stated in the by-laws "shall be to provide a means whereby all interested persons seeking spirituality in the Sahaj Marg system of Raja Yoga can come together in the name of the Shri Ram Chandra Mission and its branches for meditation and discussion."

Why are there no fees or charges for the spiritual training?

How can anyone be charged for being given what they already possess? Sahaj Marg says that spirituality cannot be sold any more than the sky can be sold, for no one owns it.

SRCM holds that anyone over eighteen years of age who is ready, willing, and able to sincerely practice Sahaj Marg may do so without any requirement to pay fees or pressure to make "donations." Sahaj Marg is available to anyone, regardless of caste or class, education, religious background, color, language, or gender.

Then how is the Mission financed?

Largely by the contributions of those who wish to give, and to a very small degree by the sale of SRCM literature. Things are kept as simple and natural as possible, but it is a fact that money is necessary to build ashrams or structures in which thousands of abhyasis can gather to meditate, to help with the costs of Master's almost constant travel, and to publish and distribute literature. There are no paid positions within the Mission. All work is done voluntarily.

Regarding donations, Lalaji was very clear: We are to look after the needs of our family and children first, and if we have any surplus, then it may be put to good use. The common sense approach of Sahaj Marg precludes impulses of overeager individuals who wish to donate all their material possessions to some group or guru. Inevitably, these sincere but misled individuals then become dependent on others and a drain on society in general. Such dramatic gestures are unnecessary, and are often escapist in their wish to throw off all duties and responsibilities onto another.

A disciple is not allowed to be childish, and a true Guru will never do for us what we must do for ourselves.

How are Mission funds accounted for?

As noted already, Sahaj Marg is registered in many countries, and in each, the legal requirements and fiscal accountability are scrupulously followed. In the United States, for example, SRCM-USA is a non-profit corporation registered in California, Georgia, New York, Texas, and Ohio. The Mission as an organization has a wealth of professionalism in its members, whose number includes accountants, attorneys, business executives, and computer experts. The Mission has retained the services of independent auditors and legal professionals on an as-needed basis to audit its policies and procedures in compliance with all federal and state laws. The books are audited yearly both internally and by an outside source and a report filed to the members at the annual general body meeting. The organization fully respects the laws of the land and full compliance is ensured at all times.

What exactly makes a place an SRCM "center"?

In India there are many towns and cities where meditation halls and offices are maintained by the local abhyasis as a gathering place to meditate. At this time in Europe and America, however, wherever there is a preceptor in a city who conducts group meditation, then his or her place of residence usually becomes a Sahaj Marg center for spiritual training. However, abhyasis may come together in any place of their convenience and meditate even where there is no preceptor present. So the term "center" can describe any place where Sahaj Marg is being practiced, even if only one abhyasi is there.

One could truthfully jest that Sahaj Marg is an entity whose Divine center is everywhere.

What is a Sahaj Marg Ashram? How often should abhyasis visit the Ashram?

The ashrams of Shri Ram Chandra Mission are reserved for meditation and training. Ashrams (Master says the word means "ultimate good") are places of work and rest for all practitioners of Sahaj Marg to visit whenever they are able. Generally speaking, only the few abhyasis necessary to maintain the physical upkeep actually live in an ashram.

Outside of India at the present time, there are only a few SRCM ashrams. Abhyasis who are able to schedule some time at an ashram should definitely do so whenever possible. Whether the Master is there physically or not, all SRCM ashrams are spiritually charged locations, and the effect of staying at an ashram can unfold for weeks and months after a visit. Holidays spent at ashrams regain their original meaning as "Holy Days." Children are welcome. Fees are minimal. Guests should please first check with the abhyasis managing the ashram before visiting.

Generally abhyasis try to come to the ashrams to celebrate the birthdays of the three Masters. The birthday of Lalaji is celebrated worldwide at Basant Panchami (the fifth day of Spring as it occurs on the Indian lunar calendar, usually in late January or early February). The celebrations for Babuji occur each year on April 30, and Chariji's birthday is celebrated on July 24. These gatherings are well-attended and last for three or four days.

SOCIAL ISSUES

I do not see how Sahaj Marg relates to my entire life. My job and family demand much of my time and energy. I have other interests and activities when I am not working. How does Sahaj Marg fit into such a busy life, one filled with many other interests and concerns?

Sahaj Marg begins as a practice and gradually becomes a way of life. When we begin, Sahaj Marg is a set of spiritual practices that we try to accomplish, a method or technique. After some time, we begin to see that everything that we do is part of our spiritual sadhana or practice, not just the times that we sit in meditation. This realization marks the beginning of Constant Remembrance, and Sahaj Marg, the Natural Path, becomes not just a practice, but a natural way of living.

Therefore, Sahaj Marg considers ordinary life the best arena for spiritual practice, and values balance and skill in all areas of life. Spirituality is not one of the compartments into which we often divide our lives — family, career, romance, health, leisure, and so on. True spirituality includes all these "compartments" and embraces every aspect of our lives.

Put another way, we might see the spiritual and material aspects of our lives as complements, not competitors. As a bird needs two wings to fly, Babuji used to say, so the human being needs two wings of existence, the spiritual and the material. If either is neglected for the other, life becomes exaggerated and unnatural. Neglect of the material existence results in dependence, and neglect of the spiritual results in a fundamental unhappiness. To realize complete perfection, we must balance both sides of our lives, and treat everything that comes our way as part of our spiritual practice.

Of course, we all have full schedules. We are all busy. But who is so busy that he cannot find time to eat or sleep or observe any of the other needs of the physical body? Just so, we must honor the needs of the spiritual body. Meditation, prayer, service, and other activities are just as essential and natural to spiritual well-being as the ones we accept without question regarding our physical life.

We must look at our priorities with honesty. No matter what we profess, our real goal is simply that which we think about most and what we value most. And what we value most, we will do — it is that basic. If you want to know what you truly value, then simply examine what you do, and what occupies your mind.

Sadhana is easy once we realize what is important. And once we realize this, time or the lack of it ceases to be a problem, for we accomplish every task before us with ease and grace. This is not a promise, but the experience of every serious abhyasi.

I come from the other extreme. I would like to do away with all my material goods and become a spiritual hermit! I would like to meditate all the time, and be with Master constantly. Will Sahaj Marg allow this approach?

Sahaj Marg suggests an even higher and more difficult approach. It is easy to be a holy man sitting on the top of a mountain, but what about being a holy person right where you are, in a traffic jam or at the office or in other such unglamorous and unromantic settings?

Please examine your expectations about what a spiritual person should look like. Sahaj Marg does not feel that the traditional paths of wandering mendicants, frocked monks and nuns, sky-clad sannyasins, and isolated hermits are suitable for everyone. Indeed, Sahaj Marg would prefer spiritual adepts to earn their living and contribute to society through normal, ordinary work and not live off the alms of others. To become a saint while raising a family and holding down a job seems impossible to the mind steeped in romantic assumptions about what saints are supposed to be and do. But such saints are being realized today in Sahaj Marg.

I feel I am not doing anything for humanity by just sitting and closing my eyes. How do I develop a true attitude toward social issues? Does Sahaj Marg encourage activism in politics or community? Does SRCM maintain any social outreaches, such as schools or hospitals or programs for the poor?

First, how do you know you are not doing anything for humanity by meditating? After some time, you may discover that your efforts in meditation resonate in many realms. Mystics and sages have unanimously found that the truest, most profound political change always comes from within, from the realization of a single individual. One has only to glance at history to verify this in the figures of Moses, Christ, Krishna, Rama, Mohammed, Buddha, and so on. Such spiritual attainments, as the life of every saint demonstrates, are not for the individual alone, but for all of us. And though we may not be saints ourselves, the spiritual practice we're able to accomplish will also bring benefit to those around us, perhaps in ways we may never know. As Master says, rice gets cooked not for its own benefit, but for others to eat.

Second, responding to the felt needs of our community, nation, and planet is considered a natural duty in Sahaj Marg. Why should it be elevated into a holy imperative only for spiritual saints or seekers? Just as looking after one's family is a normal, natural duty, so is assisting the extended family of the planet, and indeed the planet itself. But first things first.

At this time (1996) SRCM maintains no schools, hospitals or other outreaches. At some point in the future, it may. A beginning is already underway with the introduction of a curriculum in selected schools in India emphasizing a value-based spiritual education.

What does Sahaj Marg feel about the caste system in India, or the treatment of women there?

Sahaj Marg does not recognize a caste system in India, nor does it condone sexism or racism in any country. All people are welcomed by Master as abhyasis and all are treated equally according to their individual needs. Though Sahaj Marg does not recommend flouting social customs, such customs may be disregarded when they become unnatural or motivated by fear and ignorance.

Why are there no women Masters in Sahaj Marg? Is Sahaj Marg another patriarchal system?

Some who see the Master as only a man, or see him surrounded by men, tend to make this judgment. But from the level of the heart, Sahaj Marg is neither a patriarchy nor a matriarchy — it is beyond both. A sister put it this way: "I have always thought of myself as being a soul first and, incidentally, one who is also female. As I was growing up I always felt that my work in this life would be that which pertained somehow to my soul, and it never occurred to me that my being female would either hinder or help me in that work."

It is true that so far, no woman has become the Master or Representative in the brief lifespan of Shri Ram Chandra Mission. It is also true that there is no commandment which precludes this possibility at some future time, if Nature demands it. But for now, as Babuji has plainly said, the specialized duties and functions of the Master are better suited for a being who is currently incarnated as a male.

As for spiritual advancement, there are no limits for women, just as there are none for men. Indeed, Master has said again and again that women have most of the advantages when it comes to spiritual sadhana. A cursory look at SRCM will reveal that many preceptors and Centers-In-Charge are women.

One final comment on the gender of the Master. At the Cosmic level, God, or God's manifestation as the Master, may be understood as the only male principle, and all other beings as female. As Chariji once explained: "In the eyes of God, there is no male, there is no female. This is a difference in the body that is here. In the eyes of the Lord, He is the only male — all of you are females. This is the old idea of the *purusha* of the male and the devotees who are his beloved's lovers. And so it brings a certain measure of equality to the sexes, which politically or by feminist movements will never be possible to achieve."

What if a woman feels a romantic attraction to the Master?

This is not unusual. When this feeling develops and is not handled properly by the spiritual guide, it has caused the downfall not only of the unfortunate female disciple, but also of the guru and sometimes even entire spiritual communities. Therefore the selection of an honorable guide is a prime necessity — not only for women, but also for men. As Vivekananda observed, "Usually without a guru these yoga practices lead to lust, but with one this seldom happens."

Since the Master currently has a male body, it is generally females who experience the problem of physical or romantic attachment. Male abhyasis can more easily retain the classic approach of Lover-and-Beloved in the spiritual realm, but if their Master were incarnated in female form, no doubt the brothers might be asking this question, if they were brave enough!

As one sister points out, sexual feelings or dreams about Master could mean a lot of things. It could mean that Master is cleaning or regulating or otherwise doing work on our sexual system. It could mean that he is doing work in one of the "higher" points that reflect at the "lower" level. Perhaps the best start is to acknowledge that you have had these feelings, observe them, and allow the Master to make them sublime. If they persist in troubling you, you may wish to request a sitting with a preceptor. Finally, do not hesitate to write to Master about anything that is vital to your spiritual practice.

I am concerned that my children get an exposure to the religion of my culture. Can I let them go to my church or temple?

Yes.

What is the significance of offering prasad *in Sahaj Marg? I am not from a Hindu culture and this seems ritualistic to me. Is there any difference between prasad in Sahaj Marg and the prasad offered in Hindu temples?*

Traditionally, *prasad* (which means "grace") is food or drink that is offered to the Deity in a Hindu temple, and is eaten by the devotee as a means of purification and communion with God. Naturally the custom has more significance for abhyasis from that background than for Westerners, though Christians might also appreciate the value placed on charged or holy food through the sacrament of Holy Communion. Many traditions recognize the connection between physical food and spiritual food, and have various ways of acknowledging this connection.

Though from the outset it may seem ritualistic, in Sahaj Marg, prasad is given at times of celebration as a way of communing with the Master who has blessed it. At the very least, it is a charming ritual, and for a practice as lean as Sahaj Marg, it is nice to have at least one cultural reminder of the traditions from which it arose. It is also possible that prasad blessed by a Guru is a physical form of spiritual transmission, highly charged and presented in a manner that can transmute even the physical body of the recipient.

The abhyasi is free to choose either attitude. If the idea of taking prasad really bothers you, let it go. The custom of taking prasad is not essential or integral to Sahaj Marg practice. It is simply another way to receive grace from the Master.

I do not wish to get married, yet Sahaj Marg is called the householder path. Can an abhyasi remain single?

Yes. *Grihastha ashrama*, or the benefit of family life as a spiritual practice, is a description of Sahaj Marg, not a prescription. Abhyasis are always encouraged to think for themselves.

I like to date. What is wrong with unmarried sex?

For an abhyasi, all aspects of life are sadhana. What is perfectly acceptable for someone who is not in spiritual training may not be advisable for one who is. It is like an Olympic athlete saying, "I like pizzas and milkshakes. What's wrong with that?" Nothing is wrong with it for someone who is not training to win an Olympic medal. You must choose what is helpful toward your Goal. For a Sahaj Marg abhyasi, only the deepest, truest part of his own heart can make this choice.

It is simple. Look into your own heart. Whatever hinders or delays your Realization, drop. Whatever assists you in your training, maintain.

*I am homosexual, and I have been hurt that my church /
former guru condemned me. Please tell me what Sahaj
Marg has to say about homosexuality. Can a homosexual
practice Sahaj Marg?*

The response to the previous question applies to all,
homosexual or heterosexual. The only requirement to
practice Sahaj Marg is willingness, a deep longing to become
one with the Source. Beyond insisting the general truth that
spiritual attainment is impossible without moral and ethical
purity, Sahaj Marg is silent on matters regarding an
individual's sexual or financial practices, allowing and
trusting each individual's own heart to reveal the truth. All
are from God, and with His grace, all may return to God.

*Why can't I eat meat? I am not from a Hindu culture, and I
see nothing wrong with it.*

Again, Sahaj Marg does not enforce any extrinsic
discipline. If you live in a place where this is possible, you
might as an experiment go on a vegetarian diet for one year,
and observe for yourself whether it has the spiritual benefits
our Masters claim. Sahaj Marg recommends a vegetarian diet
for spiritual training wherever it is feasible to avoid meat.

*Can a serious abhyasi occasionally take a social drink or
smoke marijuana or use other "recreational" drugs?*

No. A serious abhyasi should stay in training.
Intoxicants of all kinds (this can even include disturbing or
exciting words or images) disturb the fine clarity of mind that
is achieved through steady practice. If Master gives

permission to an abhyasi to take a drink, then he or she may do so.

But I thought there were "no do's and don'ts" in Sahaj Marg!

From outside, it is true that there are very few "do's and don'ts" in Sahaj Marg. From inside, to the honest abhyasi, there are many. It is an irony of spiritual reality that the higher one advances, the more "do's and don'ts" there are. At first, we confuse mere animal license with true spiritual freedom. Later, we begin to appreciate the invertendo that absolute freedom arises only through absolute obedience to Divine Will. Till then, we are to some degree the slaves of arbitrary whims and low-order drives.

OTHER QUESTIONS

What is "invertendo"?

"Invertendo," a term coined by Babuji, refers to the fact that truth is multi-levelled, and shifts or reverses as we move from one level of consciousness to another. What at first seems contradictory becomes a paradox, and what seems paradoxical becomes invertendo.

For example, at a seminar, there may be abhyasis from many different countries. All we have to do is examine our passports to verify that it is so. At a higher level, this is inverted and no longer true. Now the truth is that there are only human beings present, male and female, young and old, tall and short, and so on. At a still higher level, there is no male/female, young/old, and so on; now the truth is that there are only individual souls carrying various samskaras. At the next level, there are no longer individual souls, for here the truth is that all are One. As for levels that may be beyond this, we cannot speak.

What does Sahaj Marg have to say about abhyasis going to psychiatrists or to Twelve Step programs if they feel they are necessary?

Sometimes it happens that buried or unresolved issues arise during an abhyasi's practice which might best be dealt with in a therapeutic setting with a doctor or qualified counselor. Abhyasis are advised to use common sense and seek help at the level help is needed, be it physical, emotional, or spiritual. If you break your leg, for example, please see an orthopedic doctor, not a guru.

I am on medication for stress reduction. Can I meditate?

If your doctor is aware of your meditation and approves, yes. Please inform your doctor and follow his or her directions.

I have a chronic illness (AIDS, cancer, a heart condition, etc.). Can I meditate?

Yes. Again, please check with your doctor. If you have a temporary fever or are injured and unable to sit, you should not meditate. Please use common sense and take care of yourself. Sahaj Marg does not require us to become martyrs and masochists.

Sometimes during meditation or when getting sittings I have felt physical pain in my heart or at other points in the body. Does this mean that spiritual work is going on?

It could. It could also mean that you have heartburn if the pain is in your chest, or if it is in your legs, it might mean that you should readjust your posture. It might even mean that you have a physical problem that needs medical attention. Generally speaking, we look to the most obvious interpretation for such physiological responses to Raja Yoga practice — that is, to the body itself.

It is also a fact that physical sensations are commonly felt in our practice. Transmission ultimately works to transform all three of our bodies, the physical (*shtula sharir*), subtle (*sukshma sharir*), and causal (*karana sharir*). These bodies might be likened to vapor, water, and ice — they are all densities of Divinity, and what occurs in one can be reflected in another. Many abhyasis, for example, report tingling feelings in the scalp or at certain points. Sometimes limbs seem to "disappear." Sometimes the body may feel vast; at other times, atomically small. These and many other somatic phenomena are generally due to the growing sensitivity to the subtler bodies as they respond to transmission.

I know people who can't sleep if they don't meditate for a day. Will I become dependent upon the practice? I don't want to become addicted to it!

After several years of practice, abhyasis can become quite sensitive to their daily condition, and will feel keenly when they are out of balance. But if people become addicted to meditation, then something is amiss in their approach to practice. It is absolutely true that we must take a single-pointed interest in our goal, but interest does not mean addiction.

Two points pertain here. First, in Sahaj Marg, meditation is a means to an end, not an end in itself. Second, Sahaj Marg meditation is not an escape from pain. True meditation is no picnic, and involves a whole series of deaths and rebirths as we confront our own addictions and relentless patterns of samskara. This is another reason why the services of a Master are so necessary for the spiritual practitioner.

In short, the practice of Sahaj Marg is not addictive. It is the means of liberation from addiction.

You say that Sahaj Marg is a dynamic system. Does this mean that the practice as we know it today may be changed or revised by the Master, or by future Masters? What about "curvature"?

The practice of Sahaj Marg has already undergone several adjustments and fine tuning by both Babuji and Chariji, and there is no reason to expect that such adjustments will not be made in the future. A living tradition will always be responsive to the needs of the time. After all, the method exists only for the benefit of abhyasis, and not the other way around, and abhyasis' needs will always come first.

"Curvature" is a term popularized by Ouspensky, although Babuji Maharaj says that Lalaji also expressed the same idea of the gradual warping away from Original Purity over time in many traditions. Curvature as such really has no relation to the "dynamic" quality of the practice.

The method of Sahaj Marg will always be embodied by the living Master, the Representative who is currently incarnated. It is the duty of the living Master to decide when aspects of Sahaj Marg practice should be changed, if at all; it is the duty of the abhyasi to obey his Master's suggestions. Abhyasis honor the entire *parampara* or lineage of Sahaj

Marg Masters by obeying the current Representative, who alone speaks with a living voice for all the Masters.

Thus, Sahaj Marg will always remain dynamic, and the practice will continue without curvature for hundreds of generations.

PART TWO

THE BASICS AND BEYOND

THE DAILY PRACTICE OF SAHAJ MARG

Morning

Say the Prayer (given below) once and sit in meditation for an hour with the thought that Divine Light is present in your heart. Do it in quite a simple and natural way without any forceful effort to concentrate. It is not necessary to visualize or see the Light — simply begin with the thought of Divine Light. There is nothing else for the mind to do. Continue meditating in one posture with your mind resting in the idea of Divine Light in the heart. When other thoughts arise, simply withdraw your attention from them.

Evening

Sit for half an hour with the suggestion that Divine Light or Energy is flowing into you from the front, washing all complexities, impurities, darkness, or grossness out through your back in the form of smoke or vapor. Do not meditate on what is leaving, but on the Divine Grace that is flowing into you. Finish with the conviction that the cleaning is complete, and that you are now filled with Light.

Prayer

> *O Master! Thou art the real goal of human life.*
> *We are yet but slaves of wishes, putting bar to our advancement.*
> *Thou art the only God and Power to bring us up to that Stage.*

Just before going to sleep at night, offer this prayer. Sit with a feeling of devotion and repeat the prayer within. Then meditate over its true sense and try to get lost in it.

THE TEN MAXIMS OF SAHAJ MARG

1. Rise before dawn. Offer your prayer and meditation at a fixed hour, preferably before sunrise, sitting in one and the same pose. Have a separate place and seat for worship. Purity of mind and body should be specially adhered to.

2. Begin your meditation with a prayer for spiritual elevation, with a heart full of love and devotion.

3. Fix up your goal which should be complete oneness with God. Rest not till the ideal is achieved.

4. Be plain and simple to be identical with Nature.

5. Be truthful. Take miseries as divine blessings for your own good and be thankful.

6. Know all people as thy brethren and treat them as such.

7. Be not revengeful for the wrongs done by others. Take them with gratitude as heavenly gifts.

8. Be happy to eat in constant divine thought whatever you get, with due regard to honest and pious earnings.

9. Mold your living so as to rouse a feeling of love and purity in others.

10. At bedtime, feeling the presence of God, repent for the wrongs committed. Beg forgiveness in a supplicant mood, resolving not to allow repetition of the same.

THIRTEEN PRINCIPLES

The following are "Principles as given by Lalaji" and were recorded by Babuji in his diary on August 17, 1944.

1. One should engage oneself in the care and upbringing of the children in such a way that it does not affect one's heart, and their love should not result in pain.

2. One should make his wife a helper, and consider oneself as one of the two wheels of the household cart.

3. One should develop such relations with the people in the neighborhood that they would seem to be one's own, and they in turn should consider him so. The same principle should hold good in the case of friends.

4. Connections with relatives should be established in such a way that the inner bond should appear severed. However, one should be a partner in their joys and sorrows. This should be with everybody. Refrain from entering into monetary transactions. When they are in dire need, financial help should be given to the extent

that one does not feel sorry if the money is not returned, and relations are not strained.

5. Behavior toward the higher officers should be such that they do not feel the principle of subordination being violated. Whatever is available in return should be considered as coming from God.

6. Opinion should not be given where it is not heeded or respected. It is not advisable to prescribe medicines in serious cases unless one is a doctor.

7. One should take service only to the extent that one is able to requite. Force of circumstances is a different matter.

8. One should never tell one's secrets to anybody. At the same time, others should not feel that some secrets are being held back.

9. One should lead a simple and selfless life.

10. As far as possible one should remain away from anxiety. Even if it comes, it should be considered as God-given, and one should remain thankful.

11. In matters of eating and drinking, one should be moderate. Due consideration should be given to pure food.

12. One should surrender everything to the Guru. Here, it is not money that is hinted at. And everything of the Guru should be considered as one's own.

13. Behavior toward the brethren of the satsangh should be pleasing and conducive to their progress. Direct opposition is very bad.

"If one follows the above principles, his life would become glorious and the world will never appear a dismal place."

— Babuji

EIGHT OBSERVATIONS

These were given by Lalaji on July 31, 1944, and Babuji recorded them in his diary with this introduction: "Master told me the following things to be observed during Bhandara, or Spiritual congregation."

1. Everyone should respect others.

2. The question of high and low should not arise.

3. Nothing should be done which is disliked by others.

4. One should desist from uncultured behavior.

5. One should keep his mind steady.

6. One should not indulge in unnecessary argumentation and useless criticism. One should ask only relevant questions.

7. The real purpose of a Bhandara is to refresh our memory of the one whose festival is being observed.

8. There should no differentiation between the gurus or disciples of other institutions and one's own.

FIFTY HINTS FROM BABUJI

from the sayings and writings of the Master

*These may be taken up individually for daily contemplation
or for consideration at group satsangh*

1. The only purpose of human existence is to realize one's nature, which is Divine. What is the goal of man? God, only God.

2. One should aspire for the highest. Peace and other things should be secondary.

3. Meditation is attention to Reality. The active and full attention should be there and not passive receptivity.

4. Thoughts during meditation are like children playing on the road. They are leaving their field waiting for Divinity to come in. One should not worry about the thoughts that rise during meditation or at other times. They rise for the sake of fall. It is not possible to become completely thoughtless.

5. After finishing meditation one must look to one's condition. This helps develop sensitivity.

6. One must be regular in practice. If interest in meditation is created, half the work is done.

7. Abhyasis should follow the Master with wisdom.

8. It is not possible to eradicate anger completely, as it is bestowed by God. One should make right use of it. But greed is our own creation. It should be eradicated completely. One should not have greed even for spirituality.

9. One should control one's freedom of action. The Ten Maxims are meant for this purpose only. Liberation is freedom from freedom.

10. Abhyasis should have control over little things of the daily routine. If not, how can they expect to have control or command over big things?

11. Chaste life should be preferred at all costs. There should be moderation in all matters.

12. Three things should be yours: your Master, your Method, and your Mission.

13. Abhyasis should not entertain the idea of becoming a preceptor. If anybody has the idea of rendering service to the mission, there are other ways by which he can serve.

14. Think that Master is Divinity while you meditate. Put bad thoughts before the Master.

15. One should avoid laziness. Great empires in the past saw their decline due to the laziness of the rulers.

16. Some respectable distance should be maintained between the male and female abhyasis. They should not mix freely as they do with members of their own sex.

17. Why should we remember God? So evolution will take place. What is evolution? The growth from animal to man, and then from man to Divine.

18. Self becomes great when it merges into Great Self.

19. Simplicity is the life of Nature. Everyone should imitate it. Greatness lies in humility and meekness. Every abhyasi should develop these qualities.

20. Movement gives growth and growth stops movement. In Sahaj Marg we start from the mind and go beyond.

21. Three obstacles in the path to Realization: 1) we try but there is no attempt; 2) we try too many things at the same time; 3) we do not have confidence in ourselves.

22. What is Yoga? A permanent realization of His presence in you, about you, and around you. Yoga is the perception of Reality.

23. Grace is the sweetness of the heart.

24. I cannot live without the Master and He cannot display without me.

25. The milder the thought, the stronger the will.

26. In spirituality gaining is losing. We do not really gain anything. Everything is in you. Lose the bad habits and gain spirituality.

27. Idle mind leads to nowhere. Searching mind grasps the material object. Quiet mind reaches to its own source.

28. Disease and illness are the operation of Nature to remove impurities.

29. Love is the awakening to Reality.

30. Philosophy is the way of thinking. Yoga is the way of doing. Realization is the way of undoing.

31. Really we have to ungrip the individuality to reach the true state of Being — Nothingness.

32. Every soul has its own identity and each soul continues to transmigrate till liberated. Life really is the awakening state of Being.

33. Definition of man: "Man is the hallucination of Being."

34. Previous lives, past lives and astronomy are but the offshoots of Knowledge. Reality is far behind. These things produce a sort of ripple in the calm water. So you are right to divorce them.

35. From two to four in the mornings is the time when it is easiest to enter the state of samadhi. Samadhi is not necessary for evolution.

36. When a man goes from one condition to another, he develops a feeling of stagnation. This is because a

buffer comes at every stage in our system of sadhana. When real condition begins, people start leaving practice. This is bad luck.

37. Trust crossing its own boundary becomes faith; faith when it crosses its own boundary becomes love, and love when it crosses its own boundary becomes surrender.

38. When idea crosses its boundary, it becomes thought. When thought crosses its boundary, it becomes intuition. Remembrance of God is the best thing. I want heart like Indians and brain like Europeans.

39. The West will be spiritualized in a shorter time than India.

40. We come from spiritual points. Prophets come from Mahamaya, a region of powerful electricity. All prophets have been born in Asia. Now prophets will be born in Europe and America.

41. Men die to become Gods. Gods die to become men. Defects in the saints: They become Masters before they become disciples.

42. In most systems the disciple must submit to the Master, but in Sahaj Marg the Master submits to the disciple.

43. We should not say that we are slaves of God. It is blasphemy to say that God produces slaves.

44. When you are angry, look at the sky.

45. Treat equally your friend and foe. That is, wish both of them well. Tolerate even if one utters a thousand curses on you. Do not fear. Master is always with you under all circumstances.

46. Mania of friendship should be given up. Selfless friends are rare in this world. For a disciple there is no friend other than the Master.

47. To increase happiness is easy — just reduce the necessities. Only one who is happy in all circumstances is truly happy. Comfort comes from without. Peace comes from within. Develop the habit of remaining joyful under all circumstances.

48. Everything can be achieved by love. Meditation and other practices are of very little importance in comparison to this.

49. It is my idea that if thought is explained, it loses its value.

50. Never mind if the whole world is against you, and your kith and kin forsake you. Be firm. Even if the sun bursts, and the skies fall upon you, do not swerve from the path you have taken up.

51. The first writer of the world had no quotations.

LINEAGE OF THE MASTERS

SAMARTH GURU MAHATMA
SHRI RAM CHANDRAJI MAHARAJ
OF
FATEHGARH

Lalaji, as he is known affectionately, was born in 1873 in Fatehgarh, U.P. The founder or Adi-Guru of the Sahaj Marg system lived as an ordinary family man and attained the heights of spiritual perfection. Lalaji is said to have re-discovered the technique of pranahuti, the yogic transmission of Divine Energy, which he was able to pass on to his successor after he left his body and entered *mahasamadhi* in 1931.

SHRI RAM CHANDRAJI MAHARAJ
OF
SHAHJAHANPUR

Babuji, who by coincidence also bore the name of his Master, was born in Shahjahanpur, U.P. in 1899. He too was a simple family man, and was known to all as Babuji, since he worked as a *babu*, or clerk. Babuji simplified the classical procedures of Raja Yoga into a system he named Sahaj Marg, or the Natural Path. He established Shri Ram Chandra Mission in 1945 in honor of his Guru, and appointed preceptors to assist spiritual seekers. When he took mahasamadhi in 1983, the Mission had already grown from his modest home in Shahjahanpur to all of India and across the globe.

PUJYA SHRI PARTHASARATHI RAJAGOPALACHARIJI

Chariji, as he is known among abhyasis, was born near Madras in 1927 and is the current Master of Sahaj Marg. Chariji is a man of considerable intellect and learning, and speaks more than a dozen languages. He worked for many years in business, but from age thirty-six his heart belonged to the old man he met in Shahjahanpur. By the time Babuji named Chari as His successor, he was already traveling and working tirelessly to bring Sahaj Marg to people all over the world. Chariji has since brought his Master's message to thousands of seekers, and for those who can see he continues to be a living demonstration of the Goal of Sahaj Marg.

GLOSSARY

Combined from the glossaries of various Sahaj Marg books

ABHYAS: Practice.

ABHYASI: Aspirant; one who practices yoga in order to achieve union with God.

ADI: Original.

ADI GURU: Original Guru; Lalaji, in Sahaj Marg.

ADI TATTVA: Original element.

ADITYA: The Sun.

ADITYA HRIDAYAM: A Sanskrit chant praising the sun; a prayer to the Sun God. (From the *Ramayana*.)

ADVAITA (ADWAITA): State of unity (Non-duality).

AGAMIC INITIATION: Initiation according to the Agamas. The Agamas are a body of spiritual literature dealing with temple rituals, temple architecture, etc.

AGNI: Fire, the fire element or principle.

AGNI NAADI: The fire naadi.

AGYA CHAKRA: See AJNA CHAKRA.

AHAM: The ego; I.

AHAMTA: Egoism.

AHAM BRAHMASMI: I am Brahma.

AHAMKARA (or AHAMKAR): Ego.

AHIMSA: Non-violence.

AIKYA: Oneness, unity.

AIKYA BHAVA: Feeling of oneness.

AJAPA: Meditation without utterance of any mantra.

AJNA CHAKRA (or AGYA CHAKRA): The fire point located between the eyebrows. Trikuti.

AKARTA: Non-doer; one who does not do.

AKASHA: Space, sky. The space element or principle.

AKASHA NADI: The space, or etheric, nadi.

AKSI: Reflected condition.

ANAADI: Without beginning.

ANAHAT: Sound which cannot be heard. Literally, "not hit."

ANANDA (or ANANDAM): Bliss.

ANANDAMAYA KOSHA: Sheath of bliss.

ANANT: Infinity or endlessness.

ANANT-KI-OR: Towards Infinity

ANANSUYATMAKA BUDDHI: Mind free of jealousy.

ANASUYA: One who has no jealousy.

ANDA: Egg; Macrocosm.

ANGAS: Limbs.

ANORANIYAN: Smaller than the smallest.

ANNAM: Food.

ANNAMAYA KOSHA: Physical sheath or food sheath (matter).

ANTARYAMI: The God within; the In-Dweller.

ANUBHAVA: Intuitional perception or personal experience in the realm of Nature or God.

ANUBHAVA SHAKTI: Intuitive capacity, capacity acquired by experience.

ANUMANA: Hypothesis, hypothetical.

ANUSHTANAM: Performance of daily rituals.

AP: Water or water principle.

APARA BRAHMAN: Determinate Absolute (see Saguna Brahman).

APARIGRAHA: Non-covetousness.

APPA: Father; affectionate term, like papa. Equivalent to the Hebrew *Abba*.

ARHAT: One of the qualifications of Gautama the Buddha. One who is fit; one who deserves.

ARJUNA: To whom Krishna gave the *Gita* in the *Mahabharata*

ASAN (or ASANA): Posture.

ASABDA: Soundless, non-verbal.

ASHANTHI: Disquiet, having no peace.

ASHRAM (or ASHRAMA): "Ashram" comes from the Sanskrit "Shreyas" which applies, in the spiritual sense, to the growth of benefits which are connected to the higher level. An ashram is also a kind of refuge, a place of retreat from today's life. Ashrams in Sahaj Marg are dedicated to meditation only, all other activities are normally not allowed in the Ashram. An Ashram is usually charged by the Master, who creates a special atmosphere of spirituality in which we meditate.

ASHTANGA-YOGA (or ASHTANG-YOGA): Patanjali described yoga as having eight limbs: yama, niyama, asana, pranayama, pratyahara, dharana, dhyana and samadhi.

ASTHEYAM: Non-stealing.

ASUYA: Jealousy.

ATMA CHAKRA: Heart chakra. In Sahaj Marg, the second, or soul, point.

ATMAN: Soul

ATMANAND: Bliss of soul.

AVADHUTA (or AVADHOOTA): Generally revered as elevated souls, but are really persons with spiritual aspirations who have become "fixed" at a certain level because their development has been arrested.

AVAKASHA: Time.

AVARANA (or AVARAN): Layers of grossness; coverings.

AVASTHAS: Conditions, states.

AVATAR: Incarnation of a Divine soul.

AVYAKTA GATI: Indifferent state. State where man is completely liberated from Maya limitations. Inexpressible condition.

AVIDYA: Ignorance.

AYODHYA: Birthplace of Lord Rama.

BASANT PANCHAMI: Fifth day of spring in the lunar calendar. It is also Lalaji's birthday.

BHAAVA: Attitude of mind.

BHAJAN: Chanted prayer.

BHAKTA: Devotee.

BHAKTI: Devotion.

BHAMUK: Illusion.

BHANDARA: A spiritual gathering or celebration.

BHARAT (or BHARATA): Lord Rama's brother.

BHAVAS: Expression of an inner condition; attitudes of the mind.

BHISHMA PITAMAH: Grand uncle of Pandavas and Kauravas in the *Mahabharata*.

BHOG (or BHOGA, or BHOGAM): Process of undergoing effects of impressions; experience; enjoyment.

BHRUMADHYA: Between the eybrows.

BHUH: One of the states of consciousness.

BHUMA (or BHOOMA): Absolute; Ultimate; Base.

BHUMIKA: Stage in spiritual evolution.

BHUVAH: One of the states of consciousness.

BISMIL: Auspicious beginning.

BODH: Wisdom.

BRAHMAN (BRAHM): Center; God; Ultimate.

BRAHMACHARYA: Student phase of life; celibacy, literally "like Brahman."

BRAHMA-GANDHA: Divine smell.

BRAHMAGATI: Divine state, state of Brahman.

BRAHMA-KAMA: Love of God; desire for God.

BRAHMA LOKA: World or realm of the Divine.

BRAHMANDA (or BRAHMAND): Astral world. Cosmos.

BRAHMANDA MANDAL (or BRAHMANDA DESH): Mental sphere, supra-material sphere, cosmic region; sphere where everything manifests under a subtle shape before taking place in the material world.

BRAHMANDI SUR: Celestial vibrations.

BRAHMARANDHRA: A point or opening in the crown of the head.

BRAHMA-RASA: Divine pleasure, enjoyment, or taste.

BRAHMA-SABDA: Divine sound.

BRAHMA-SPARSA: Divine touch.

BRAHMOPADESHA: Initiation; teaching of higher knowledge about Brahman.

BHRUVORMADHYA: Point between the eyebrows, used in certain Yogic systems as a point for concentration.

BUDDHAM SARANAM GACCHAMI: "I seek refuge in the Buddha."

BUDDHI: Intellect.

CAKRA: See CHAKRA.

CENTER-IN-CHARGE: The person responsible for overseeing the spiritual and administrative work of Shri Ram Chandra Mission in a country, or in a region of India.

CHAITANYATA (or CHETANYATA): Consciousness, including a subtle activity.

CHAKRA: Center of super-vital forces located in different parts of the body; figuratively called lotus.

CHELA: Student or disciple.

CHIT (CHITTA): Consciousness.

CHIT LAKE: Another name for Brahmanda Mandal.

CLEANING: 1. Specific meditation done at the end of each day by all Sahaj Marg abhyasis. 2. Use of will power by the Master or preceptors in utilizing pranahuti to remove subtle distortions (vikshep), coverings (avarana) and impurities (mala) that impede an abhyasi's development.

DAKSHINA: South; also offering by disciple to Guru for training received.

DAKSHINAYANA: The six months of the sun's southern path.

DAM: Control of senses and indriyas.

DARSHAN: Vision of someone's inner Reality.

DEVA VANI: Divine voice.

DEVATA: A god; Cosmic personality.

DEVI UPSAKA: A Devi (Mother-Goddess) worshipper. Tantrik worship.

DHARANA (or DHARNA): Mental focus (sixth limb of Patanjali's yoga).

DHARMA: A term with many applications, depending on the context: Duty; righteousness; destined way; truth; virtue; that which upholds.

DHARMAJA: One born of righteousness. Also, first-born child.

DHARMAKAYA: The dharma body, body built of righteousness.

DHOTI: A long cloth worn by men around the waist.

DHI: An element of sama*dhi*; *sama*, meaning balance, and *adhi*, meaning original or ancient. See samadhi.

DHRUVAGATI: State of Dhruva.

DHRUVA (DHRUV PAD): Highly evolved soul. First or lowest level of cosmic functionary. Below the Druvadhipati.

DHRUVADHIPATI: Godly functionary of great caliber who directs the work of the Dhruvas. Below the Parishad.

DHYANA (or DHYAN): Meditation (seventh limb of Patanjali's yoga).

DIKSHA: Initiation.

DURGA CHAKRA: Durga plexus.

DVAITA: Duality.

DVANDVA: Dualities; the pairs of opposites (e.g., good-bad, pleasure-pain).

EKAGRA VRITTI: Tendency to fix our attention on one thing at a time.

FANA: A spiritual condition. Also, destroyed or sacrificed.

GADDI: A mattress for sitting on the floor. In politics, the expression "to aspire for the gaddi" means to seek to be the leader of an organization.

GANGA YAMUNI: A level of transmission from Lord Krishna.

GAYATHRI: Shri P. Rajagopalachari's home in Madras, named after the Gayathri mantram.

GAYTHRI UPADESH: Teaching of the Gayathri mantra.

GITA: Divine knowledge given to Arjuna by Lord Krishna in the Mahabharata. Also, the *Bhagavad Gita*, or "Song of God," an essential scripture of Hinduism, containing a portion of the epic *Mahabharata*.

GRANTHI: Knot.

GRIHASTHA (or GRAHASTHA): One who leads a worldly life, a householder.

GRIHASTHA ASHRAMA: Conditions of a household life.

GUNAS: The three qualities of nature in Hindu philosophy: *Sattva, rajas* and *tamas*.

GURU: Master who transmits light, knowledge; a spiritual teacher.

GURU DAKSHINA: Fee due to the guru for training received.

GURUMAT: Disciples who obey the commands of the Master in all matters and try to submit to his will in all possible ways. Note: Do not confuse with GURU MATA which is the common name given to the Guru's wife.

GURU PASHU: People who become devoted to the Master's physical form.

GURU STHAN: The place where the guru sits during satsangh.

GYANA: See JNANA.

GYANI: See JNANI.

HANUMAN: Lord Rama's faithful servant in the Ramayana.

HARIJAN: Children of God; fifth caste.

HATHA YOGA: The first four stages of Patanjali's ashtanga yoga. The practice of Yoga concerning the body.

HAVAN: Offering of an oblation with fire. Also called Homa.

HINDI: Language of North India.

HIRANYA GARBHA: A golden fetus; the name of Brahma the Creator; a soul invested with sukshma-sharira, or the subtle body.

HYLEM SHADOW: Spiritual shadow located to the right side of the sternum.

HRIDYA CHAKRA: Heart plexus.

INDRIYAS: Ten senses/organs of Indian philosophy, subdivided as jnana and karma indriyas. The former are five senses pertaining to perception, knowledge or wisdom, while the latter are five senses pertaining mainly to action.

INTRODUCTION: Refers to the introductory sittings given to all who begin the practice of Sahaj Marg.

INVERTENDO: Term coined by Babuji to describe the apparent inversions Truth undergoes as it moves through higher levels of abstraction.

ISHA: God, as Ruler.

ISHWARA (or ISHWAR): Determinate Absolute. God as Existence endowed of all the most subtle attributes.

ISHWARI MANDAL: Determinate Absolute's region.

JADA SAMADHI: Lower levels of samadhi.

JAGAT GURU: World teacher.

JALA: Water; the water element or principle.

JAL-DAN: Prayerful offering of water.

JAMILA: Actor in a drama.

JANAH: One of the states of consciousness.

JANMA: Birth.

JAPA: Repetition of a mantra.

JAYANTHI: Birth anniversary.

JIVA (or JIVATMA): Individual incarnated soul. Life.

JIVAN MOKSHA: Liberation while alive in the physical body.

JNANA: Supreme Wisdom or Knowledge leading to Realization.

JNANA BHUMIKA: Stage or state of knowledge.

JNANA HINATA: Absence of knowledge or unknowledge.

JNANI: Gnostic; one who has Divine knowledge.

JYOTI: Splendor, effulgence.

JYOTIMAYA: Form of effulgence.

KABIR: Ancient Indian Poet

KALAKSHAPAKA: A person who wastes time.

KAMA: Desire; love.

KANTHA CHAKRA: Throat plexus.

KARANA SHARIR: Causal body.

KARMA: Action.

KARMA INDRIYAS: Organs or senses of action.

KASBI: Acquired condition.

KAYASTHA: Name of a caste.

KOSHA: Sheath. The five sheaths that contain the essence and together comprise a human being are the food-sheath, breath-sheath, mind-sheath, knowledge-sheath, and bliss-sheath.

KRISHNA (or LORD KRISHNA): Most recent incarnation of Vishnu; divine personality in *Mahabharata*.

KRISHNA-CHAKRA: Divine weapon.

KRIYA: Action.

KRODHA: Anger.

KSHIPTA: Disturbed condition of mind due to sensations such as hunger, thirst, anger, sorrow, desire of fame and wealth.

KSHOBH (or KSHOBHA): State of disturbance; loss of equilibrium; stir caused by the will of God to effect creation. The original stir.

KUNDA: Referring to the Kundalini; also, a bowl-shaped vessel.

KUNDALINI: The power which is coiled like a serpent at the base of the spine.

KURUKSHETRA: The battlefield in the *Mahabharata*.

KUTCHA: Unfinished, raw.

LAGAN: Attachment.

LAYA: Dissolution.

LAYAVASTHA: The state of merging.

LILA: Divine play.

MAHABHARATA: One of the epic stories of India.

MAHAH: One of the states of consciousness.

MAHA KALA CHAKRA (or MAHA KAL CHAKRA) Supreme's Wheel. (See footnote in *Towards Infinity*, discussion on Seventh Knot).

MAHAMAYA: Subtle energy used by the Divine—Great Maya or great illusion. The spiritual sphere from which avatars come.

MAHA NIRVANA: Illumined state.

MAHA PARISHAD: The highest cosmic functionary; Ruler of the Universe.

MAHAPRALAYA: State of complete dissolution when everything in existence merges with the Center. The complete dissolution of the whole universe.

MAHA SAMADHI: The final samadhi when a saint renounces his body and enters the brighter world.

MAHATMA (or MANAMATA): Great soul, saint.

MAHATO MAHIYAN: That which is greater than the greatest.

MAL (or MALA): Impurities.

MANAS: Psyche, mind.

MANASA LAKE (MANASAROVAR): Another name for the Brahmanda Mandal.

MANI PADMA: The jewel in the Lotus.

MANMAT: Disciples who approach a guru for worldly, material goals.

MANOMAYA KOSHA: Mind sheath.

MANTRA (MANTRAM): Recitation of a sacred sound, word, or phrase.

MATH (MUTT, MATHA): Spiritual organization.

MAYA: Phenomenal appearance. It is really a power of God. All manifestation or expansion which seems illusory is the play of Maya. Illusion.

MOKSHA: Liberation or Salvation. But in Sahaj Marg, both are not the same. "Freedom from bondage is Liberation. It is different from Salvation which is not the end of the process of rebirth."

MOODHA: Condition of the mind, including the tendencies which cause laziness, indolence and idleness.

MUDRA: Yogic "seal" or secret practice. Also refers to certain postures and hand gestures.

MUHURTAM: Auspicious moment.

MUKTI: Liberation.

MUMUKSHU: A seeker of the spiritual Truth.

MUNI: See RISHI.

NABHI (NAABHI): Navel.

NADI (NAADHI): Commonly refers to the pulse beat; subtle channels; any physical tubular organs in the body

NAMASTHE (NAMASKARAM): Greeting, a salute to the God within.

NARADA: A Divine sage.

NIRAKAR: Formless.

NIRGUNA: Without attributes or qualities.

NIRGUNA BRAHMA: Indeterminate Absolute. The Ultimate Cause.

NIRMANAKAYA: A created body.

NIRODHA: Tendency which brings the mental to a state of perfect self-control, free of all complexity and perturbation.

NIRVANA: Illuminated state.

NIRVIKALPA SAMADHI : Samadhi in which we are not conscious; ecstasy with the loss of the world-consciousness; consciousness of abstract.

NISHKAM: Desireless.

NISHKAM KARMA: Desireless action.

NISHKAM UPASANA: Desireless devotion.

NIVRITTI: Retrogression; destructive return or withdrawal.

NIYAMA (or NIYAM): Subjected laws which must be followed. They are purity, contentment, austerity, self study, self abandonment (devotion to God).

NYASA: Something entrusted to another, put in trust.

OJAS: Splendor.

OMKAR: The sacred syllable "Aum" (OM).

OM SHANTI (OM SANTIH): Invocation of peace.

PANCH AGNI VIDYA: Wisdom of the five fires (see footnote in *Towards Infinity*, discussion on Fifth Knot).

PANCHA BHUTAS: The five elements or principles in Hindu cosmology: earth, water, fire, air, and space.

PANCHAMAKAARA: The left-hand path, also called Vaamchaara — an esoteric and occult practice of Tantrik schools. They use Matsya (fish), Mamsa (meat), Madhya (alcohol), Mudra (position of fingers during religious worship), Maithuna (copulation) — all beginning with "M" or "Ma," and since there are five of them it is called the Pancha-makaara, or "Five Ma's."

PANDAL: Tent.

PANDIT: Learned person, well versed in any subject.

PARA BRAHMAN (or PAR BRAHMA): Indeterminate Absolute; God as the Ultimate Cause of Existence.

PARA BRAHMANDA: Supra-cosmic consciousness.

PARA BRAHMANDA MANDAL: Supra-cosmic region of the mind.

PARAMANUS: Subtle particles.

PARISHAD: Cosmic functionary below the Maha Parishad who directs the work of the Dhruvadipatis.

PASUS: Generally refers to all living things; specifically, to animals; most specifically, to cows.

PATANJALI: Ancient Indian scholar who wrote the Yoga Sutras.

PINDA (PIND): Material or gross existence, that which exists in the gross or material state.

PINDA DESH (or PINDA PRADESH): Material sphere; the heart region.

PITRI BHAVA: Paternal feeling.

PRABHU: Master; God.

PRABHU-PRAPANNA: Spiritual condition experienced as being both the Master and one who has surrendered.

PRADESHAS: Conditions, states.

PRAKRITI: Nature.

PRALAYA: State of dissolution, applied not to the whole universe but only to a part of it.

PRAMANA: Authority, or valid means of knowledge.

PRANA: Life, breath.

PRANAHUTI: Process of yogic transmission; derived from prana meaning life and ahuti meaning offering. Offering of the life force by the Guru into the disciple's heart.

PRANAM: Respectful salutation; obeisance.

PRANAMAYA KOSHA: Breath sheath.

PRANA PRATISHTA (or PRAN PRATISHTA): Power to infuse a spiritual force into a picture or idol.

PRANAVA: The syllable "Aum."

PRANAVA JAPA: Chanting the "Aum," or pranava.

PRANAYAMA: Derived from prana (life, vital force) and from ayama (to restrain). The regulation of Prana.

PRAPANNA: A spiritual stage; also, one who has surrendered.

PRAPTI-VIRODHIS: Enemies of our attainment.

PRARABDHA: Fate, destiny.

PRASAD (PRASADAM): Divinized food, usually sweet; an offering to Master or God.

PRASTHANA TRAYEE: The three orthodox scriptural books of the Hindus; viz., the Upanishads, the Bhagavad Gita and the Brahma Sutras.

PRATYAHARA (or PRATYAHAR): The inner withdrawal of the mind (fifth branch of Patanjali's Yoga).

PRATYAKSA: Present before one's vision or eyes.

PRAVRITTI: Progress (constructive); upward growth.

PRECEPTOR: An abhyasi chosen, prepared, and permitted by the Master to impart spiritual training through the utilization of pranahuti or yogic transmission.

PRITHVI: The earth; earth element or principle.

PUCCA: Ripe, complete.

PUJA: Religious traditional practice (in Sahaj Marg, the meditation practice).

PUJYA: Revered, respected; used as an honorific at the beginning of a great man's name.

PUNYA: Righteous or meritorious action.

PURUSHARTHA: The goal of the human effort — applied in the same time to the purely human goals or the supra-human goals.

PURVA KARMA: Past actions, and their effect.

RAJA YOGA (or RAJ YOGA): Ancient system or science followed by the great rishis and saints which helped them to realize the Self or God. Usually used for meditative practices, as distinguished from hatha yoga.

RAJA DASHARATH: (Surya dynasty) Father of Rama.

RAJA JANAK: Father of Seeta (or Sita).

RAJAS: One of the three Gunas. Leads to activity, egoism and selfishness.

RAM (or LORD RAMA): Husband of Seeta in the Indian epic story Ramayana.

RAMAKRISHNA: Saint who lived in Calcutta at the end of the nineteenth century and who was Vivekananda's Master.

RAMANUJA: One of the three acharyas; founder of the Vishishtad-vaita system of Vedanta Philosophy.

RAMAYANA: One of the epic stories of India.

REPRESENTATIVE: In Sahaj Marg, a term reserved for that person who is nominated by a Master as successor; the currently incarnated Master and president of Shri Ram Chandra Mission.

RICHA: Cosmic recording of all thoughts and events.

RIG VEDA: One of the Vedas. The others are YAJUR veda, SAMA veda and ARTHARVANA veda.

RISHI: Saint; seer; one who has realized Self.

RUDRA SHAKTI: Destructive power; power possessed by a rudra of whom Shiva is the personification.

SADGURU: Guru capable of giving the knowledge of Truth.

SADHAK: Disciple who practices a sadhana.

SADHANA: Spiritual practice.

SADHANA CHATUSHTAYA: The four-fold spiritual practice: *viveka* or discrimination; *vairagya* or detachment; *sampatti*, meaning to be engrossed in it, and *mumukshutva*, to seek liberation.

SADHU: Religious or spiritual person.

SAGUNA: With gunas or characteristics, qualities, and attributes.

SAGUNA BRAHMAN (or SAGUNA BRAHMA): God as Existence endowed of all the most subtle attributes. Determinate Absolute.

SAGUNA ISHWARA: Determinate Absolute; having the quality of Ishwara.

SAHAJ AVASTHA: Natural state or condition.

SAHAJ MARG: Natural path, simple path.

SAHAJ SAMADHI: Natural samadhi, considered the highest samadhi: simultaneity of total external awareness with total inner emptiness or absorption.

SAHASRA DAL-KAMAL: Lotus of a thousand petals. Chakra at the top of the head.

SAHEB: A respectful form of address to a man.

SAKAR: Tangible form.

SAKHA: Friend.

SAKHAYA: Friendship.

SAKTI DIVINE: Highest energy.

SAKHYA BHAVA: Friendly feeling.

SALOYA: In the same world as another.

SAMAAN: Similar.

SAMADHAN: State of self-settledness to the Master's will.

SAMADHI: Original balance. State in which we stay attached to Reality. In Sahaj Marg, the return to the original condition, which reigned in the beginning. Babuji split the word into *sama*, meaning balance, and *adhi*, meaning original or ancient.

SAMARTH GURU (or SAMARTHA GURU): A perfect guru, who possesses all the qualities. A perfectly balanced guru.

SAMAVASTHA (SAMATVA): A balanced state.

SAMIPYA: Nearness.

SAMPATTI: A type of human realization. In Sahaj Marg it is also the depth of the spiritual realization.

SAMSKARAS (or SANSKARS): Impressions; grossness.

SANDHI GATI: Merging of two states.

SANDHYA: Meeting point between day and night.

SANG-E-BENAMAK: A lump of salt from which saltiness has been taken away.

SANKALPA: An act of will.

SANKIRTANISTS: Those who do sankirtan.

SANKIRTANS: Congregational chants.

SANNYASI (or SANNYASIN): One who has renounced the world and leads a solitary life of celibacy and asceticism.

SANSKRIT: Culture; also name of the ancient language of India.

SANSTHA: Spiritual tradition; organization; group.

SAPTA-BHUMIKA: Seven stages.

SARASWATI: The goddess of learning.

SARUPYATA: State in which we acquire the same form.

SARVAMUKTI: Simultaneous universal emancipation.

SARVAM KHALVIDAM BRAMHA: "All this is but Brahman." A Vedic statement.

SAT: Being, Reality, Existence.

SATPAD (or SATYAPAD): In Sahaj Marg, state which is neither lightness nor darkness. It is a reflection of the reality which itself is still further.

SATSANGH (SATSANG): 1. Spiritual assembly. 2. Being with reality.

SATSANGHI: One who attends satsangh.

SATTVA: One of the three gunas. Leads to balance or poise. It manifests in virtuous conduct and brings about happiness.

SATTVIC: Pertaining to or that which promotes sattva in the body.

SATYAM: One of the states of consciousness. Also means truth.

SATYODAYAM: The dawn of reality.

SARUPYA: Similarity; become one with; having similar form and appearance.

SAYODAYAM: The dawn of reality.

SAYUJYATA: Close conformity; something identical; become one with.

SHABDA (SHABD or AJAPA): Sound, inner vibration within, as opposed to japa.

SHAKTI: Power.

SHAMA (or SHAM): Peaceful condition of the mind leading to a state of calmness and tranquillity; the first of the *shat sampatti.*

SHANKAR: Shiva, one of the Trinity in Hinduism, the others being Brahma and Vishnu.

SHANKARACHARYA: Ancient saint of India, who propounded advaita.

SHASTRAS: Holy books (scriptures).

SHAT: Six.

SHAT SAMPATTI: Six forms of spiritual attainments in the third Vedantic Sadhana.

SHATCHAKRAS: The six chakras or plexuses, symbolically denoted as lotuses, situated in the subtle body. They are:
1. Muladhara, or root chakra, at the perineum
2. Svadhidhtana, at the genitals
3. Manipuraka, navel
4. Anahata, heart
5. Vishudha, throat
6. Ajna, center of the eyebrows

SHIKAR (SIKHAR): Crown, top, summit.

SHITHALI: One which endows with coolness.

SHRADDHA: Faith; devotion with faith.

SHRAMDAN: An offering of physical labor.

SHRISHTI: Era of Creation in the Indian calendar.

SIDDHIS: Capacity to do miracles; powers.

SIDDHOPAYA: Readily accessible. Also, ready means.

SIKHAR: Crown, top.

SITTING: A session of meditation, usually lasting from 30 minutes to an hour, in which the Master or a preceptor meditates with a group or an individual for the purpose of cleaning and transmission.

SRUTI: The basis of each musical note. Also the Vedas or revealed scripture.

STHITAPRAJNA: One who is established in the Self. Alternatively, one whose consciousness in merged in the Self.

STHULA SHARIR (or STHOOL SHARIR): Gross body.

SUKSHMA SHARIR (or SOOKSMA SHARIR): Astral body, subtle body.

SUDARSHAN CHAKRA: Lord Krishna's finger wheel.

SUDDHA SATTVA BODY: Pure body.

SUPATRA: Well-deserving person.

SUSHUPTI: One of the four states of consciousness. It is described as the consciousness of deep sleep in which a man does not dream. When this state of mind is attained, a man gets in close communion with God, though he remains in a forgetful state.

SRUTI: The basis of each musical note. Also, the Vedas, or originally revealed scriptures.

SVAR: One of the states of consciousness.

SVADISTHANA CHAKRA: The chakra located at the level of the genital organs.

SVADHYAYA: Study of holy scriptures combined with practice.

SWAMI VIVEKANANDA: See VIVEKANANDA.

SWAMI: A Hindu priest. Saint.

TAM: The actual state we were in when the world was born. Real state of being.

TAMAS: One of the three gunas. Inertness. It leads to inactivity, sloth or procrastination.

TANUM SWAM VIVERNUTE: Reveals its own form.

TAPAH: One of the states of consciousness.

TAPASYA (TAPAS): Ascetic practices to purify the soul and attract Divine grace. Literally means "heat," and indicates the heat generated by the friction of intense spiritual practice.

TARKA: Reasoning.

TATTVAS: Elements or principles in Hindu cosmology. (See PANCHA BHUTAS.)

THAS: Condition of total grossness.

TILAK: Pigment mark on the forehead.

TITIKSHA: State of fortitude or forbearance.

TRIKUTI: The point above the nose between the two eyebrows; one of the points of concentration.

TURIYA: Fourth state of consciousness, the other three being:
1. Jagrat, the waking state,
2. Svapna, the dreaming state,
3. Sushupti, deep sleep.

TURIYA AVASTHA: Fourth state of the soul, when it becomes one with God.

TURIYATITA: Beyond the turiya condition.

UPADAM KARAN: Cause which itself results in effect. Thus it may be explained as root cause. See KSHOBH.

UPADESH: Sermon. Instruction.

UPADESHAK: Instructor, advisor.

UPANAYANAM: Opening of the higher eye.

UPANISHADS: Vedantic part of the Vedas (Jnana Kanda).

UPARATI: Self-withdrawal.

UPASANA (or UPASNA): Devotional practice.

UTSAV: Religious celebration.

UTTARAYANA: Six month's of the sun's northern path.

VAIRAGYA: Renunciation, detachment.

VASANAS: Past impressions

VASU: Another name for Krishna. Also refers to cosmic functionary below the Dhruva, an elevated person who performs the lowest level of godly work entrusted to him.

VAYU (VAYA): Air or air principle

VAYU NADI: The air nadi.

VEDAS: Ancient Indian scriptures, in which a superior knowledge is revealed.

VIDYA: Knowledge; science.

VIJNANAMAYA KOSHA: Sheath of knowledge.

VIKSHEPA (or VIKSHEP): Distraction, confusion.

VIKSHIPTA: Refers to the tendency which drives the mind away from sacred thoughts and brings about the haunting of numerous irrelevant ideas at the time of meditation.

VIRAKTA: Recluse.

VIRAT: Cosmic.

VIRAT DESH: See BRAHMANDA MANDAL.

VIRAT ROOP: Cosmic form.

VIRYAM: Virility; strength.

VISESA: Specific object or quality.

VISHNU: One of the Hindu trinity, God as preserver.

VISHUDDHA CHAKRA: One of the six chakras or plexuses, situated at the base of the throat.

VISHVARUPA DARSHANA: Vision of the Lord's Cosmic form.

VIVEKA: Discernment.

VIVEKA SHAKTI: Power of discrimination.

VIVEKACHUDAMANI: A text written by Adi Shankaracharya.

VIVEKANANDA (or SWAMI VIVEKANAND): A great saint of India who lived in the early twentieth century, and was a disciple of Ramakrishna.

VRITTIS: Outward flow of mind; subtle desires or stimuli coming up in the mind causing action; mental tendencies.

VYAVAHARA: Connection between people; behavior.

YAJNAS: Religious rituals, sacrifices.

YAKSHA: A class of semi-divine beings; a living supernatural being.

YAKSHA PRASNA: Series of questions asked by a yaksha to Dharma Putra in the *Mahabharata*.

YAMA: 1. Self interdiction. Vow of abstinence of violence, falsity, robbery, unchastity, and tendency to acquire. 2. Lord of Death.

YATRA: Voyage; journey; pilgrimage; the inner spiritual process.

YOGA: A system of Hindu philosophy showing means of emancipation of the soul from further migration.

YOGA JA: Intuitive perception of all objects. One who is born from the yoga practice.

YOGI (YOGIN): One who practices yoga; one who achieves union with the Absolute.

YUJ (YUJA, YUJYA): To join or unite; to yoke.

BIBLIOGRAPHY

Chandra, Ram (Babuji). *Complete Works of Ram Chandra: Volume I.* Pacific Grove, CA: Shri Ram Chandra Mission, 1989.

——. *Autobiography of Ram Chandra: Volume II.* Shahjahanpur, India: Shri Ram Chandra Mission, 1986.

Chandra, Ram (Lalaji). *Truth Eternal.* Shahjahanpur, India: Shri Ram Chandra Mission, 1986.

Durai, A.P. *Basics of Sahaj Marg Sadhana: Questions and Answers.* Pacific Grove, CA: Shri Ram Chandra Mission, 1992.

Feuerstein, Georg. *Encyclopedic Dictionary of Yoga.* New York: Paragon House, 1990.

——. *Holy Madness.* New York: Arkana, 1990.

Gupta, M.M. *Jewels of Sun: Sayings of Babuji Maharaj.* New Delhi: M.M. Gupta, 30 April 1987.

Levine, June, ed. *Shri Ram Chandra Mission Golden Jubilee Commemoration 1945-1995.* Madras: Shri Ram Chandra Mission, 1995.

Mascaró, Juan, trans. *Bhagavad Gita.* New York: Penguin Books, 1962.

Rajagopalachari, P. *Heart to Heart: Volume II.* Pacific Grove, CA: Shri Ram Chandra Mission, 1991.

—————. *Letters of the Master, Volume III.* Pacific Grove, CA: Shri Ram Chandra Mission, 1996.

—————. *Principles of Sahaj Marg: Volume 1.* Shahjahanpur, India: Shri Ram Chandra Mission, 1986.

—————. *Principles of Sahaj Marg: Volume 8.* Shahjahanpur, India: Shri Ram Chandra Mission, 1994.

—————. *Principles of Sahaj Marg: Volume 9.* Shahjahanpur, India: Shri Ram Chandra Mission, 1995.

—————. "Inevitability of Spiritual Evolution." *Constant Remembrance: The Spiritual Quarterly of Shri Ram Chandra Mission,* XII, no. 1 (January 1996): 2-8.

Sarnad, S.A. *In the Divine Presence of Shri Babuji.* (In manuscript.)

Sogyal Rinpoche. *The Tibetan Book of Living and Dying.* San Francisco: HarperCollins, 1992.

Vivekananda. *Inspired Talks*. New York: Ramakrishna-
Vivekananda Center, 1987.

————. *Raja Yoga*. New York: Ramakrishna-
Vivekananda Center, 1982.

————. *The Yogas and Other Works*. New York:
Ramakrishna-Vivekananda Center, 1984.

INDEX OF QUESTIONS

Page numbers appear in parentheses

7. Are other motives acceptable in practicing Sahaj Marg? For example, will it cure my physical illnesses? Will it help me with depression? Will it have a positive effect on my career and earning potential? I'm not sure about this "Self-Realization" stuff; I just want peace and relaxation. Is this acceptable? (20)

8. How can we tell if we are progressing toward the Goal? (21)

OTHER WAYS

1. How does Sahaj Marg compare with other systems? (23)

2. I am a Christian. Does this mean I am converting? Should I stop going to church? Can't one be Christian or Hindu or Buddhist and also be an abhyasi? Must I give up my religion? (23)

3. I am an atheist. Must I believe in God to practice? What does Sahaj Marg say about reincarnation? Is it necessary to believe in reincarnation to do this practice? (24)

4. What is the relation between Sahaj Marg and Raja Yoga? (24)

5. What about Karma or Bhakti or Jnana Yoga? (25)

6. What about Hatha or Vinyasa Yoga? (26)

7. What about Nada or Taraka Yoga, Kriya Yoga, and Tantric or Kundalini Yoga? (26)

8. I am already practicing some meditation; why can't I just do both Sahaj Marg and another practice? (27)

7. I have too many bad habits to start a spiritual practice at this time. Much as I might like to, I'm afraid that I cannot leave my vices. (39)

8. I think I might like to give the system a try, but at this point I cannot promise that I will stay with it forever. Is this acceptable? (40)

9. Why are we asked to devote three to six months to test the practice of Sahaj Marg? (41)

10. How exactly are we supposed to tell if the practice is working? What changes should we expect during this trial period? (41)

11. What are the suggested guidelines for the trial period? (43)

12. I have noticed that many of those who begin Sahaj Marg in the West do not even stick with it for the initial three months. Why do they leave? (45)

THE MASTER

1. What does the term "Master" mean in Sahaj Marg? (48)

2. How does one recognize a Master of caliber? (50)

3. What is the role of the Master? (52)

4. I feel that the idea of a Master somehow comes between me and God. Why must we have a Master? Can't everyone go to God directly, without any intermediary? (52)

5. But I still do not like the idea of having to depend on some external authority figure and giving them power over me. (53)

5. Are the introductory sittings not considered initiation? Does initiation exist in Sahaj Marg? If so, why does Master initiate some abhyasis and not others? (67)

6. Please describe the yatra, or journey. How do we know our position or approach, that is, at which point we are supposed to be? (68)

MORNING MEDITATION

1. What is so special about meditating at dawn? What if my work or family schedule does not permit this? (69)

2. How is Sahaj Marg meditation different from just sitting silently and trying not to have thoughts? (70)

3. Please explain what is meant by "the Divine light in the heart" we are supposed to meditate upon. How is this done? What are we supposed to see? (71)

4. You say we begin with an initial thought or *sankalpa,* and then we sit with an attitude of inner attention. This sounds similar to Zen *shikan taza* ("simply sitting") *zazen* meditation or Yogic *vipassana* (witnessing or insight) or even Tibetan *dzogchen* ("great perfection") meditation. Is Sahaj Marg meditation like these — or, how is it not? (73)

5. Can I play music during meditation? Can I meditate with my eyes open? Can I try and think of good things? Can I lie down and meditate? Can I chant a mantra? (74)

6. What about the place where I meditate. Is having a special room for *puja* (worship or meditation) necessary or helpful? (75)

PRAYER

1. Why pray? I thought Babuji said, "Prayer is begging, meditation is having"? (87)

2. The first line of the Mission Prayer bothers me because I do not like praying to a human being, but only to God. (89)

3. The second line of the Mission prayer bothers me because it sounds like a negative affirmation. (89)

4. The third line of the prayer: Why does it say "the only God and power"? Why is the Master equated to this? (90)

5. Please explain the distinction between the cleaning meditation to remove samskaras and the use of the Tenth Maxim. (90)

CONSTANT REMEMBRANCE

1. Why "Constant Remembrance"? I prefer "Constant Presence" or "Constant Mindfulness." "Remembrance" seems like a reference to the past. I feel we should be in the present only. (92)

2. We are told to think that Master is doing whatever we happen to be doing, not ourselves. But how can I imagine Master doing bad things or having bad thoughts? (93)

PRECEPTORS

1. Why does the Master need preceptors to help him? (95)

2. How often should I attend satsangh? Is it a requirement? (104)

3. I do not like groups. Can't I practice on my own and just get individual sittings? Is it really necessary for me to attend group meditations? (105)

4. Are there any rules or programs for satsanghs? For example, should there be readings from books or talks by abhyasis? I find that satsanghs vary from place to place and do not seem to have any set pattern. (105)

5. Why must we wait for several hours before and after satsangh to have individual sittings? (106)

6. What is the technique we should use in group meditations? Is it the same as when receiving individual sittings? (107)

7. Why do men and women sit separately in satsangh? (107)

Keeping a Diary

1. I do not like writing. Is keeping a diary essential? What are the reasons to keep a spiritual diary? (108)

2. What sorts of things are we supposed to write in our diary? (108)

Writing and Visiting Master

1. Can one meet the Master personally? How accessible is he? (110)

THE MISSION

3. Why are there no fees or charges for the spiritual training? (116)

4. Then how is the Mission financed? (116)

5. How are Mission funds accounted for? (117)

6. What exactly makes a place an SRCM "center"? (118)

7. What is a Sahaj Marg Ashram? How often should abhyasis visit the Ashram? (118)

SOCIAL ISSUES

1. I do not see how Sahaj Marg relates to my entire life. My job and family demand much of my time and energy. I have other interests and activities when I am not working. How does Sahaj Marg fit into such a busy life, one filled with many other interests and concerns? (120)

2. I come from the other extreme. I would like to do away with all my material goods and become a spiritual hermit! I would like to meditate all the time, and be with Master constantly. Will Sahaj Marg allow this approach? (121)

3. I feel I am not doing anything for humanity by just sitting and closing my eyes. How do I develop a true attitude toward social issues? Does Sahaj Marg encourage activism in politics or community? Does SRCM maintain any social outreaches, such as schools or hospitals or programs for the poor? (122)

4. What does Sahaj Marg feel about the caste system in India, or the treatment of women there? (123)

OTHER QUESTIONS

1. What is "invertendo"? (130)

2. What does Sahaj Marg have to say about abhyasis going to psychiatrists or to Twelve Step programs if they feel they are necessary? (131)

3. I am on medication for stress reduction. Can I meditate? (131)

4. I have a chronic illness (AIDS, cancer, a heart condition, etc.). Can I meditate? (131)

5. Sometimes during meditation or when getting sittings I have felt physical pain in my heart or at other points in the body. Does this mean that spiritual work is going on? (131)

6. I know people who can't sleep if they don't meditate for a day. Will I become dependent upon the practice? I don't want to become addicted to it! (132)

7. You say that Sahaj Marg is a dynamic system. Does this mean that the practice as we know it today may be changed or revised by the Master, or by future Masters? What about "curvature"? (133)

SAHAJ MARG TRAINING CENTERS

As of January, 1996, Sahaj Marg is being practiced in more than forty countries. For names of preceptors nearest you or for information on ordering Sahaj Marg literature, please contact one of the centers below.

North America
Shri Ram Chandra Mission
Post Office Box 269
Molena, Georgia 30258
United States

Phone: (770) 884-0888
Facsimile: (770) 884-5003

India and Asia
Shri Ram Chandra Mission
19, North Street, Sriram Nagar
Madras, 600 018, India

Northern Europe
Shri Ram Chandra Mission
Vrads Sandevej 4
8654 Byrup
Denmark

Phone: (45) 75.75.71.01
Facsimile: (45) 75.75.71.02

Southern Europe
Shri Ram Chandra Mission
Château d'Augerans
39380 Augerans
France

Phone: (33) 84.81.57.34
Facsimile: (33) 84.71.79.93

ABOUT THE AUTHOR

Clark Powell began his search for ultimate reality as a teenager. Raised as a Methodist in the Deep South, he went on to explore the charismatic practice of Christianity in the late 60's and early 70's. Later, as he read widely and studied the Eastern traditions, he began to meditate first on his own and eventually within the formal tradition of a Zen Buddhist community in California. By the time he was introduced to Sahaj Marg, he had been meditating in various traditions for some twenty years, yet was astounded by the rapid changes he found within after only a few months of Sahaj Marg practice. He was made a preceptor in October, 1992, and afterwards went to India to spend several months observing and learning at the feet of his Master. Since then, he has continued to write and work as a taxi driver while raising a family, directing the SRCM center in Mobile, Alabama, and continuing his daily practice of Sahaj Marg.